Advance Prai~
DREAMING WITH MARIPOSA~

"Sonia Gutiérrez masterfully evokes the voices of the Chicano forebearers in her debut novel, Dreaming with Mariposas. The text reads like a new song; in it you can hear the whimsical humor and self-aware candor of Sandra Cisneros, as well as the iconic vignette voice and style of the great Tomás Rivera, made anew for the contemporary audience. Gutiérrez gracefully navigates difficult themes that are relevant to today's reader, such as immigration, sexism and the search for destiny. Dreaming with Mariposas contains all the hallmarks of a new classic. I just love it!"

—Gris Muñoz, author of *Coatlicue Girl*

"Sonia Gutiérrez invites us to dream in her world made up of literary skill as we follow the mundane and the miraculous ways migrant families exist in the United States. She brilliantly humanizes these experiences as we get to know Sofía and Paloma; two brown girls growing up in North County San Diego. Gutiérrez provides a window of opportunity to understand transregional knowledge of border life between San Diego and Tijuana through a sharp lens of race, gender, class, and doctors that live in another country. She masters the use of bilingual phrases and cultural cues of Mexican and Indigenous systems of being: limpias, paletas, bikas, domingo, manzanilla, yerbitas y santos, el burro, piñatas, cebollita y cilantro, tacos y carne asada, guayaba trees, el mercadito, cholo boys, la chota y la migra. We understand the cultural complexity that Sofía and Paloma navigate as they imagine dream worlds of college aspirations. I am confident my students will revel in its familiarity and newcomers will fall in love. Without dreams, butterflies, and writers like Gutiérrez, our world would not be beautiful and delicious. These human connections are all sacred, and without them, we would not exist y punto."

—Angélica M. Yañez, Ph.D.,
editor of *United States History from a Chicano Perspective*

Dreaming with Mariposas

Sonia Gutiérrez

FLOWERSONG
P R E S S

FlowerSong Press

Copyright © 2020 by Sonia Gutiérrez

ISBN: 978-1-953447-99-9

Library of Congress Number: 2020952189

Published by FlowerSong Press
in the United States of America.
www.flowersongpress.com

Cover art by Jorge Garza "Qetza"

Set in Adobe Garamond Pro

Typeset by Matthew Revert

www.matthewrevert.com

Dreaming
with
Mariposas

FLOWERSONG
P R E S S

ALSO BY SONIA GUTIÉRREZ

Spider Woman / La Mujer Araña
The Writer's Response, 6th edition (coeditor)

For my firstborn and secondborn,
Quetzal and Paulina Xitlalli
Mendoza Gutiérrez—the power of two

Contents

"I would like to see all of the people together. And then, if I had great big arms, I could embrace them all. I wish I could talk to all of them again, but all of them together. But that, only in a dream. I like it right here because I can think about anything I please. Only by being alone can you bring everybody together."
—Tomás Rivera, *. . . y no se lo tragó la tierra /
. . . And the Earth Did Not Devour Him*

"In the meantime, in my writing as well as in that of other Chicanas and other women, there is a necessary phase of dealing with the ghosts and voices most urgently haunting us, day by day."
—Sandra Cisneros, "Ghosts and Voices:
Writing from Obsession"

Dreams

Beneath a thick blanket of smog, Dad and Mom were two butterflies taking flight. In Los Ángeles, disoriented by the honking of engines running, they navigated the busyness of city streets and dodged oncoming cars.

At home, in our one-bedroom duplex, Mom insisted our words were fluttering dreams. They began when our eyes turned off all the lights, and our imagination switched ON and visited the place of dreams. From the kitchen, Dad called it a night, "Buenas noches, Palomita y Chofi." Mom reminded my sister, Paloma, and me, "Dreams—the ones you want to come true—share them out loud with your eyes wide open, so your dreams can guide you through the world of the living." Mom whispered sweet wishes to our ears, "Que sueñen con las maripositas," made the sign of the cross, and tucked us into our twin bed as we flew to Dreamland, the place of our ancestors.

In the morning, we shared with each other our good dreams and repeated these dream stories to ourselves over and over, so we wouldn't forget. And one day, as Dad and Mom assured, our dreams would travel to us, or we would travel to them, and before we knew it, we'd be laughing, running, sitting, and even flying in our dreams.

There were other types of dreams too though—more like living nightmares—that made us wail inside. I learned those stories, even though Mom and Dad said to be polite and not to share them out loud, they had to be told. We needed to train our tongues, so they wouldn't be afraid to speak for us.

Or else it would happen again and again.

But no one wanted to hear those dream stories because people wanted to hide them in brown cardboard boxes, seal them with red masking tape, and hide them in their closets. When Paloma and I heard these stories come out and whimper with broken wings, tears ran down our chubby cheeks. And like our parents, we dreamed of better tomorrows for them and for us.

Up, Up, and Away!

We were on a plane catching up to Dad who was working in another state, and Paloma was scared holding onto Mom's arm. I wasn't. I looked out the window at the little world below me. I was up, up, and away leaving Los Ángeles like Superman, my superhero, who looked like my Uncle Miguel, Dad's dead cousin, who's here but not here, the one with a curl on the side of his forehead. We were flying on a plane—a real plane—not like Wonder Woman's invisible jet on our way to see Dad to a place called Idaho, where he was milking cows, and there were rows and rows of potato fields waiting for someone like my mom. Dad told Mom over the telephone a packing company in Boise was looking for workers who wouldn't take days off the potato line.

In Idaho, during the summer, Mother ran over snakes with her car. She made mushy guacamole and salsa out of snakes until they were really, really dead. In the winter, *I know you're not going to believe me*, but I'll tell you anyways. Paloma and I used to walk barefooted in the snow. *Really. I swear.* Idaho, that's where people spoke funny cowboy Spanish and asked, "*¿A poco estas son tus dos huercas?*"

One day, I was playing on the porch making a pot of pozole with rocks, water, and dirt when the push of a broom sent me flying off the porch. And I fell like you see in cartoons.

Like when the Road Runner pushes Wile E. Coyote off a cliff. There was a rusty nail sticking out of the wall, and it tore my arm open like an old sock. See this scar—it's shiny and feels soft. Touch it—I can't feel a thing. Mom didn't know what to do because we were home alone. I didn't cry until I saw the blood dripping on my Levi's overalls. Mom says I could have died or lost an arm because we only had one family car, and Dad had driven to the dairy to work that morning. I'll tell you what really happened: Uncle El Gordo's wife pushed me off the stairs because she thought her husband—our uncle—who wasn't really our real uncle, spoiled us. She was jealous.

I heard Mom say Uncle El Gordo had a *pre-mo-ni-tion*, a *co-ra-zo-na-da* or an *in-tui-tion* from the pit of his big fat belly, heart, mind, and soul—a living dream—a force we can't see told him to return home. *And he did.* By that time, Mom had wrapped my little arm, and Uncle El Gordo rushed us to the nearest hospital about forty-five minutes away. I was lucky I didn't lose my right arm, or else I'd be walking around left-handed *like this*.

Weeks later, when my scar got itchy, a doctor needed to check my wound and to pull out my stitches, Mom told her boss she needed to take me to the doctor for a checkup. Her boss warned, "Helena, if you clock out, you're fired!" When he talked to her with a screaming mean voice, my mom raised her right eyebrow and yelled, "Me ponch!" as she clocked out and left without her boss's permission.

Months later, Dad said, "Helena, it's too cold here! We're leaving!" And because we're a family of butterflies and can't survive Idaho's cold weather, we returned to sunny Alta California in our brand-new time machine, Mom's Monte Carlo, just in time for Dad's new job as a dishwasher where his fingers looked like my toes when I stayed in the bathtub for too long. That's why we're here in Vista, but now Dad's up north in a place called Bakersfield working construction. There's work over there. He promised he'd be back Friday night.

I forgot to tell you. My mom—she applied for *un-em-ploy-ment*, and when she explained what had happened to her to the interviewer, he got red in the face, and Mom's boss got in trouble and ended up paying her long after we left the potato fields and the sweet, sweet smell of manure.

Rocky Girls

We were far away from Idaho. In Vista, California, when we got home from school, we waited for our parents at our temporary living space while Dad and Mom saved money for our very own place, where one day we would be free. At our uncle's place, we lived in a small duplex with no space to put our backpacks. Uncle David's wife, Aunt Carlota, with big rollers in her hair and whose jealousy infected her with mean-spiritedness, kept an eagle eye on us. Their son, our cousin Poncho, must have inherited Aunt Carlota's evil spite because he'd always pick on us, and I was the target of Poncho's mischievous behavior.

When adults weren't looking, he'd either kick me or pinch me. Aunt Carlota wouldn't do anything about her son's bullying, and I—the direct hit of his discontent—was her secret victory.

For a few months, we were "Los Arrimados" at their place. And Paloma got tired of me being picked on, so she warned our cousin several times.

"Poncho, if you don't stop, I'm going to hit you. Poncho, if you don't stop—I'm going to hit you. *I'm going to hit you, Poncho.*"

And Poncho who didn't take girls seriously picked on me again and again. When Paloma gave our boy cousin her best right-handed punch in the center of his stomach, Poncho couldn't breathe. Struggling for air, he fell to the ground and curled up like a roly-poly. Immediately, we ran and hid until our parents came home even though we heard our Aunt Carlota's Doña Florinda screams, "Palomaaaa! Chooofi! Wait till your parents get home from work and find out what you did to David!" That was it. We knew we'd get punished, and we hated disappointing our parents, especially our father.

Hours later, in his cement blotched jeans and faded navy-blue T-shirt, Dad came looking for us as if he knew our secret hiding place. Staring at both of us with big honeyed eyes and taking a grip on both of our arms, he knelt and directed his words at Paloma: "Today, you hit your cousin, Poncho, because he hit your sister." He then looked at me with his deep-set eyes and continued, "And that was the right thing to do. In the future, if anyone tries to hurt you or your sister, you have my permission to hit that person back."

Dad had taken us to see the movie, *Rocky*, to the Oceanside Valley Drive-In, where we watched the película from Dad's Mexican lemon green Plymouth. He, a middleweight boxer himself, would float like a butterfly and throw his sweaty hands in the air and let us sink our small fists into his palms. We were the Martinez girls, Paloma and Sofia "Chofi," like the ch sound in *chu*-rros and *cho*-co-la-te, who had grown up with boxing, and the instinct was there—and this time—Poncho's stomach was proof. I couldn't wait for my parents to save enough money, so we could buy our own place free of Poncho and his *pinches* pinches.

Knuckles, Magic Rings, and Brushes

When it wasn't Poncho, it was Uncle David. Our uncle, my mom's brother, insisted on cracking all our knuckles—there was no escape. Our little bodies contorted like blind worms as we endured the pain. Another time he swore if we kept rubbing our index finger, a magic ring with a red ruby would appear on our finger. It did. First, in the form of cherry red peeled skin. Days later, a rich deep maroon scab took form. And finally, a permanent silky light pearl resurfaced on our magic fingers.

Other times, with his cowboy talk and chest pushed out, Uncle David would ask, "Chofi, did you brush your hair?" With my shoulders caved in and a sigh, I'd answer, "Yes, Uncle David. I really, really did brush my hair." He'd poke fun, "Again Sofia Martinez—since it doesn't look like you brushed your hair! And don't come back until your hair doesn't frizz up like an old plastic broom." My Madrina Cleo, my godmother, was my second mother just in case anything happened to Mom and Dad (like dying). "Look—Chofi already brushed her hair. Look at that," she'd add to the ridicule, by making fun and staring in amazement at my fluttering hair.

On one of those weeknights when it was time for Mom to thoroughly yank my scalp and braid my long wavy hair, a scrawny kid in Poncho's second grade class, who lived down the hill, stood at the door asking if he could go outside and play ball with my cousin. With the mere sight of the boy, I wanted Mom's bright royal blue, yellow, and bright piñata pink ribbons braided into my hair.

But nothing happened though once Mom set the braids in. The brushing I had to conform to, especially in the presence of Uncle David's shiny, parted hair. I couldn't tell Uncle David the truth I kept to myself and only told my sister. Inside I was happy that one day we would be moving to our own place, where Paloma and I could spread our wings and wouldn't have to put up with Aunt Carlota, Uncle David's pranks, and their son, Poncho.

The idea of ever having a little brother scared me. Mom had been planning a boy, and I never ever wanted to have a brother who would be mean to girls—or boys.

Things Poncho Said

After Paloma punched Poncho, he didn't hit me anymore. Instead, he pinched me with words.

"Your nose looks like—your Dad's."

"*You think so?*"

"Yeah—your mom must have cleaned your nose with a straw."

"A straw? *Really?*"

"Yeeahhhh—because your nostrils are *so big*. They're big like the holes on the moon—like the holes in Swiss cheese. Yeah— your face looks like the moon too. It's round like your nostrils."

"So—what did Aunt Carlota, your mom, clean your nose with?"

"My mom was very careful. She cleaned my nose with a cotton swab. No—she cleaned my nose with a toothpick. That's why I have small nostrils—*not like yours*. I have a pretty nose—not an ugly one. Mine isn't flat like yours."

"*Really?* My mom says I have a cute button nose."

When I looked at Poncho's nose, it didn't look any different from mine.

Paloma's Last Confession

"Bless me, Father, for I have sinned."

"What brings you here?"

"I talked back to my parents. I lied to my mom when I said my sister, Chofi, peed our bed—it was really me. I hit my cousin, Poncho—because he hit my sister first—my father said it was okay though. I hit my sister too, but she's my sister. Umm. I didn't do my homework because I like watching TV after school while our parents are at work. I saw a man and a woman kissing on TV. I like a Samoan boy at school. His name is Josh. *What else?* Umm. I forgot. Oh, yeah, I remember now. I don't like reading books because they make me feel tired and sleepy. I talked to a stranger on the street even though my mom said not to talk to strangers—that's because he asked me a question. Umm. I stole a quarter from my father's drawer. I can't think of any other sins—I think that's it."

"*Is that it?*"

"Yes, Father—I think so."

"*Little girl, do you want to go to Hell?*"

The Prayer

At Santa Fe Elementary, teachers gathered us at an assembly and quieted down our large group. Mr. Peterson, our principal, had an important announcement: "Good afternoon children, the Vista Sheriff's Department has asked me to please talk to all of you about an important issue. If your parents haven't already shared the news, the police are looking for a kidnapper . . . ."

A kidnapper? What did kidnappers do? Did they take naps with kids? Did Mr. Peterson look like a kidnapper? "Children, please make sure you do not walk home alone. I repeat. DO NOT WALK HOME ALONE. If you walk to school, make sure you walk in groups of three or more." *Could the kidnapper be the man in the white car who stared at Paloma and me and other children while we waited at the bus stop? The kidnapper. Could a father be a kidnapper? Was our old babysitter's son a kidnapper?*

For the rest of the day after the assembly, the only thing I could think was how to avoid the kidnapper. *What could I do to avoid the kidnapper?* That night I did what I had seen my mom do when she needed a special favor.

I prayed.

Dear Diosito,

This is Chofi. *Remember me?* I need your help. Mr. Peterson, our principal, says we need to be careful because a kidnapper is kidnapping children on their way to school. He says the kidnapper goes after girls, but boys need to be careful too because you never know. Like I said—I need a special favor from you, but I don't know what you'll think. Okay—here it goes.

Can you please make my chichis—my boobies—stop growing?

Lucky for me I didn't get kidnapped in elementary. But there were plenty of children's faces my age on milk cartons. The principal's talk at school made Paloma and me realize we had come across several weirdos with bad intentions, but we had never told Mom or Dad.

The Grown Man

Weeks later after we heard the sheriff's warning at school, we looked for the right time to tell Mom.

"Paloma, let's talk to Mom today about what happened in Idaho when she gets home from the factory."

"Yes, let's do that. But Chofi, you tell Mom because you're better at these things."

So, after dinner, we went on a walk down the hill to our local park on the corner of East Vista Way and Civic Center Drive to tell Mom about what had happened when we lived in Boise. Our memory was blurry, but Paloma and I still remembered. Paloma held onto Mom's right hand, and I held on tightly to her left hand. Paloma with a nod signaled that it was the right time to spill the beans and the sopa.

"Amá, we want to tell you something."

"*Girls, is everything okay?*"

"Remember, when we used to live in Idaho?"

Mom nodded with a worried look on her face.

"Amá, while you worked at the potato factory and Dad at the dairy, when we used to stay with our babysitter, the woman we called Abuelita—do you remember her?"

"Sí, Mija. ¿Qué pasó?"

"Our babysitter's son, probably Dad's age, sat at the dinner table and drew naked ladies with one of the children's Etch

A Sketch toys. When our babysitter went to the bathroom to take a shower, her son would unzip his pants and show us what looked like a pink blob and tell us, 'It's a lollipop. Lick it.'"

An awkward silence consumed our mother, Paloma, and me.

Abuelita, as we called her (We didn't really have a grandmother—only in the spirit world) didn't know her son was a cochino. A pervert. That day instinct must have told Paloma to step away—and not to—because Paloma pulled both of us away from the creep.

With a bewildered stare, Mom asked, "*Why didn't you say anything?*"

Dollars Did Grow on Trees

When Mom and Dad saved enough money together, we finally moved to our very own one-bedroom apartment in Vista on East Los Angeles Street. It wasn't our dream house, but at least we had a place of our own. And even though Paloma and I had to share a twin bed in our small living room, at least Poncho was no longer around to pick on me.

Because Paloma was older than me, she called all the shots. It never bothered me when Paloma took my loose change because she knew how to make more money. For Paloma, money did grow on trees. She, like a bird perched on a branch, could see from high above what needed to be done to convert quarters into dollars. Paloma understood the language of numbers. With her big clumsy writing, she was Mom and Dad's palomita de la suerte, their pigeon of good fortune, since my sister wrote out checks with big elementary sized letters for Mom and filled out applications for Dad. And even though our parents had Paloma fill out their paperwork, she never whined. Well, at least I never heard her complain. I remember seeing important documents stuffed in a white trash bag in the closet that made my head spin, so I was glad Paloma was my parents' firstborn and could read all the important documents with big numbers because I couldn't understand or explain them to Mom and Dad.

Paloma's almond eyes smiled when we talked about dimes, nickels, and quarters. "Chofi, if we add your quarter and my quarter, we'll have fifty cents, and then we can afford ice cream from the paletero. ¿Qué dices?" I'd nod in agreement. Paloma was good at convincing me. With that money, we bought a Neapolitan ice cream sandwich instead of sharing a Big Stick. We sat on the trunk of Dad's 73 Plymouth with gray patches and passed our ice cream sandwich back and forth while we watched children play ball and ride their bikes on the parking lot's blacktop. One day like the other children living at our apartment complex we would also have our own bika with rainbow streamers. We'd add stickers and ride it together in our neighborhood—one day.

That summer Paloma came up with the idea of starting our own ice cream business, so we wouldn't have to share ice cream sandwiches anymore. With the money we saved from our domingos, we bought Popsicle sticks and sold all types of homemade paletas. We made chocolate popsicles from chocolate milk, orange flavored popsicles out of orange pulp, water, and brown sugar. And when we ran out of ingredients in the kitchen, we added raw eggs and lemon juice with water (that was Paloma's idea—not mine). Once our paletas were frozen and ready to eat, we went door to door at our apartment complex and sold the entire batch.

The day we sold our last Lemon-N-Egg Popsicle, I cringed when our last customer, a White freckled boy with blonde hair, blurted out, "It's good!" That was the end of our summer ice cream business because Mom found out about the raw eggs. With furrowed eyebrows and piercing eyes, Mom scolded us,

"That's not right. You two should be ashamed of yourselves. Children can get sick from eating uncooked eggs. Wait till your father finds out." (Paloma and I didn't see it coming because we had seen Dad with our very own eyes drink a glass of rompope and one raw egg for breakfast.) After learning about our shenanigans, Mother fastened the red ribbon on her slip with a safety pin and took a long, long nap because she was pregnant and expecting *a boy*.

When father got home, he asked us to turn around. One at a time he forced us to lick each other's back and elbows. Paloma's back tasted rather salty. There were rules we learned from Dad and Mom to making money the right way, or else there'd be consequences.

Mother and Her Scissors

Mother was always dream making. In our second-floor apartment, not wanting to waste any cloth, Mother cut with precision with her metal sharp scissors with black handles—just like she did with her words. With each hand gesture, her scissors produced a deep baritone of seriousness. In her imagination, bright dresses for Paloma and me took form.

During weekdays, like a silent spotted kitten, I wrapped myself around her left foot until she called it a night. After a long day at Spanjan, the sewing factory in San Marcos along Highway 78, Mother bent her back to cut cloth on our small veneer dinner table and sew on her raging sewing machine. She could make something out of nothing. First, she created her own patterns out of Lucky's brown paper bags. She then made burgundy and navy-blue velvet sweatpants and sweatshirts and sold them to our friends, relatives, and neighbors because Mom and Dad were saving up money for a down payment for our dream house.

Mother knew the language of scissors—concise and to the point. She treasured her scissors more than any relationship and always carried them in her purse. In a sewing work environment fueled by competitiveness and envy over who produced more in less time—for the company—Mother remained a woman of few friends, evading gossipmongers like her coworker, Julieta, who lived in the same apartment complex as us.

Just like the day I waited for her to talk to Julieta in the parking lot at our apartments. Mother kept her sharp scissors in her right hand waist high in an *I'll shank you* position. What escaped her mouth was too far to hear for my ears. In the distance, Mother's scissors glistened in front of her coworker.

Weeks later, as she had predicted, the squawking stopped. Mother had gotten a hold of Julieta's ears, just like she firmly grasped her sharp scissors with her right brown hand.

The Mango and Mambo Days

Even though mangoes were expensive in the U.S., the smell of ripe mangoes filled our apartment. Those were the mango and mambo days because Mom was craving mango, and Paloma and I were learning to dance mambo. After a long busy week of sewing at work and cleaning a house on Saturday morning and CCD, the sounds of Pérez Prado, Lola Beltrán, *Saturday Night Fever*, Elvis Presley, Freddy Fender, Celia Cruz, Juan Gabriel, and Carlos Santana blared directly from our apartment's living room—from our consola—sitting proudly next to our old staticky antenna TV.

In our apartment, Mom was a raging sewing machine, Dad was music, and la consola was life. After breakfast, when our family completed all our cleaning chores, like deep cleaning the restroom and the refrigerator, Mom and Dad set us free. Paloma and I lifted our music console's heavy wooden lid, propped it open, and turned on the power switch. Dad gave us permission to take out his collection of black vinyl records from their jackets and sleeves while he dusted the records and placed them under the needle. With the music playing as loud as we could without disturbing our neighbors, we danced to the King of Mambo—Pérez Prado—except Mom. With the blowing coming from the golden mouths of trumpets, she trailed off with her pregnant belly to her bedroom to her sewing machine because she didn't enjoy dancing like we did.

"¿Qué le pasa a Lupita? No sé.

¿Por qué ella no baila? Su papá.

¿Qué dice su papa? Que no.

¿Qué dice su mama? Que sí.

Que baile Lupita. Sí. Sí."

Our next-door neighbors never complained about Dad's music being too loud nor did the military family downstairs complain about our dancing feet.

The music console looked more like a dresser except that instead of drawers it had a mustardy, coarse fabric, covering its front speakers. Dead cockroaches were stuck between the numbers and lines on the dashboard of our state-of-the-art AM-FM radio even after we turned the knob to push them out of the way. It didn't matter if zombie cockroaches at the disco and their dead bodies wouldn't be leaving our consola anytime soon. We still danced and sang to Dad's music collection anyway. "La música te consuela, Mija," Dad would say as he sang along to Juan Gabriel, "No tengo dinero ni nada que dar. Lo único que tengo es amor para dar." When we danced to "El Noa Noa," we just had to move our bodies like expert wobbly rubber bands.

Juan Gabriel and Dad were right.

Our console held a record for every human emotion. Music—it didn't make sense to me why some fathers didn't allow their daughters to dance before their quinceañeras.

Why didn't Lupita's dad want her to dance? Was music good or evil?

The Speech Therapist

At Santa Fe Elementary, every Thursday, Mrs. Lopez took me to a little white trailer. The English alphabet surrounding the four rectangular white walls, and her perfume choked the tiny room we sat in. The tinkering of her gold bracelets broke the silence with every hand gesture as she began her dictatorship: "*Aaa* as in a-pple. *Eee* as in e-le-phant. *Iii* as in Indian. *Ooo* is for oc-to-pus. *Uuu* is for um-bre-lla." Her tongue exaggerated the pressure against the roof of her mouth as the sounds of vowels somersaulted in my mouth as I repeated the sounds coming from hers. The red apple, the gray elephant, the Indian with the feather, the purple octopus, and the black umbrella like the one on the Morton's salt container were always the same.

I visited the trailer even though I thought I already spoke English. When words escaped my mouth, Mrs. Lopez must have heard a squeaky trumpet because I visited her office quite often. On one of those pronunciation days, Mrs. Lopez said, "Sofia, I know somebody who didn't need braces to straighten her teeth," while staring at my mouth. She continued, "All she had to do was press down on her teeth like this," while her knuckles pressed against her front teeth. That day I learned English wasn't my only imperfection. Ironically, at our new school we would be taunted for only speaking English on school grounds. At San Marcos Elementary, there would be no children like Paloma and me. Only White kids spoke English, and the children of Mexican parents born here, in Escondido or Oceanside, spoke Spanish y punto.

Laurel Trees and a Purple Building

"Helena, this weekend we're going to visit my cousin, the one I told you about who almost drowned in the Río Balsas. Do you remember my Primo Javier? He moved to Pacoima."

"Yes, I remember you said your Primo Javier had nightmares after that incident. *You think we can get there?*"

"Pacoima? Yeah, I think so. My cousin said to exit at the McDonald's next to a church with a big white cross then take a right and keep going straight until we see a row of white laurel trees and a big purple building. That we wouldn't miss it."

"Pancho, remember the last trip? All the houses, buildings, and streets looked the same. That time we got lost for almost three hours. There weren't any payphones nearby to call and get directions. And Crucito—you know how impatient the baby gets in his car seat."

"We'll make it, Vieja. Don't worry. Javier said to go to the Liquor Store with a big yellow inflatable beer and to call him from a payphone once we get there."

"Pancho, just make sure you take your cousin's phone number with us, so Paloma can call him in case we get lost. Please don't forget Javier's number. I'll get the children's clothes ready for Sunday since I have to clean a house in Rancho Bernardo on Saturday morning. You can take the girls to CCD and watch Crucito while I clean the Richardsón's house."

"Me parece bien, Helena. I'll make the tomatillo salsa my primo loves so much."

"Ándale pues, Pancho. Let's leave at six o'clock in the morning to arrive by eight to Pacoima and return before traffic hour."

El Huevo

One weekday evening Mom took an egg and blessed it in our small apartment. Then, she blessed my little brother, Crucito, with an egg and made the sign of the cross several times. For two days throughout the night, he kept waking up with a startled cry for no apparent reason because he didn't have a fever or seemed to suffer from baby colic since manzanilla would have already soothed his gas pains. *Estaba asustado.* His soul was frightened. Mom kept repeating several prayers—good prayers, of course, like the ones I learned before my First Communion while she carefully rubbed el huevo on my brother—not missing a single part of his little body.

When Mom finished the limpia, she cracked the egg carefully and dropped it into a glass of water. The yolk dropped slowly to the bottom of the glass, and some spirits dropped to the bottom, and then other spirits rose to the top of the glass. "He'll need several limpias," Mother said aloud as she observed the glass of water and the egg. *It was true*—my little brother was frightened. Mom never shared her knowledge about the egg and its healing powers with anyone like the day she talked to our new neighbor while I pretended to wash dishes.

"Do you know how to cure a child's susto?"

"Yes, neighbor."

"How do you cure them?"

"Well, with prayers, of course."

"I do the same. With 'Our Fathers' and 'Holy Marys, Vecina.'"

"Chofi, when you finish washing dishes, go ask the neighbors who live in the blue house across the street if you can get guava leaves from their tree. Make sure Paloma goes with you."

"Okay Ma."

Our Doctor Who Lived in Another Country

Whenever Paloma, Crucito, and I got so sick Mom couldn't heal us with her herb-filled cabinets, an egg, or Vaporú, we had to wait for the week to hurry up, so Dad could take us on a trip to visit our doctor who lived in another country. We crossed the border to a familiar place called Tijuana, Baja California, México. Estados Unidos Mexicanos—the United Mexican States—said the large shiny Mexican pesos in Spanish. With her miracle stethoscope, our doctor's Superwoman eyes and Jesus hands always found where the illness hid.

As our father drove into Tijuana, the city looked like an expensive box of crayons. Fuchsia and lime green colors hugged buildings. Dad parked our shiny Monte Carlo the color of caramelo on the third floor of a yellow parking facility, and we walked down a cement staircase and crossed onto Avenida Niños Héroes. Then, we went up peach marble stairs and entered our doctor's waiting room.

On the weekends, patients from faraway cities like Los Ángeles and San Bernardino came to see La Doctora. Judging from the looks of some of the patients' faces, they were there to see the doctor's husband, who was a dentist. They made the perfect couple—the doctor and the dentist—for both their Mexican and American patients. The doctor, a tall woman with smoky eye shadow, looked directly into her patients' eyes when she spoke. Not like some American doctors in the U.S. who didn't look at Mom because she only spoke Spanish.

On one of those doctor visits, I heard the dentist, a tall, burly man with a mustache that looked like a broom, speak English on the telephone with a patient. "John, you need to come in, so I can take a look at your tooth."

Another time I saw an elderly gringo, waiting for his wife, seeking the dentist's services. That's when I realized the other side was expensive for them too.

When we were done at the doctor's office, our next stop was El Mercadito on the other side of the block on Calle Benito Juárez. Churros sprinkled with sugar and cinnamon in metal washtubs rested on the shoulders of vendors. Fruit cocktail and corn carts were closer to the sidelines of streets, so passersby could make full stops and buy their favorite pleasure bombs to the taste buds.

During summer visits to Tijuana, Paloma ate as much mango as she wanted because fruit was affordable in México. My weakness was corn. And even if I felt sick, I always looked forward to eating a cup of corn topped with butter, grated cheese, lemon, chili powder, and salt. Mexican corn didn't taste like the sweet corn kernels from a tin can—Mexican corn tasted like elote.

Approaching El Mercadito, dazed bees were everywhere. Mother warned us about not harassing bees. Because according to Mom, bees were like us—like butterflies. "Without bees, our world would not be as beautiful and delicious. Bees are sacred, and without them, we wouldn't exist. Paloma and Chofi, please don't ever hurt bees," Mom said as we walked by our fuzzy relatives and nodded in agreement.

The smell of camote, cilacayote, cajeta, and cocadas added to the blend of enticing smells at the open market, where we roamed with buzzing bees peacefully. Colorful star piñatas and piñata dolls of El Chavo, La Chilindrina, and Spiderman hung along the tall ceiling, and the familiar smell of queso seco filled the air heavy with delight. Wooden spoons, cazos made of copper, molcajetes, loterias, pinto beans, Peruvian beans, and tamarindo provided such a wide selection of merchandise vendors didn't have to fight over customers. Politely, they asked, "What can I give you?" or "How much can I give you?" as we walked by.

In Tijuana, street vendors sold homemade remedies for just about anything imaginable. "This cream here will alleviate the itch that doesn't let your feet rest," and "For a urine infection, drink this tea," vendors hollered. And then there were the funny concoctions, for which even I, a girl my age, didn't believe their miracle powers: "For the loss of hair, use this cream that comes all the way from the Amazon Islands."

Hand in hand with our familia, Paloma and I walked the streets of Tijuana with our sandwich bag full of pennies and nickels. We gave our change to children who extended their little palms up in the air. Mom would take a bag full of clothing and find someone to give it to, which I never understood, because most people on the streets dressed just like us, from the pharmacists to children wearing school uniforms.

Once, when we were walking in Tijuana, Paloma and I saw a man with no legs riding what looked like a man-made skateboard instead of a wheelchair. Our eyes agreed; the man needed the rest of our change.

Besides the rumors about Tijuana being a dangerous place, nothing ever happened to our car or Mom's purse. In Tijuana, doctors had saved Crucito's life because my parents knew, if they took Crucito to a hospital in the U.S., he might not come out alive because American doctors wouldn't try hard enough for a little brown baby like my little brother. In Tijuana, our parents spoiled us with goodies and haircuts at the beauty salon. And I felt bad for Americans who couldn't afford a doctor and didn't have a good doctor or a dentist like ours in El Otro Lado—on the Mexican side. Pobrecitos gringos.

Launderland

". . . Girls—to do the dishes
Girls—to clean up my room
Girls—to do the laundry
Girls—and in the bathroom . . ."
—The Beastie Boys, "Girls"

Because we couldn't afford a fancy steam iron, Mom was very practical. Instead of using a plastic spray bottle, she sprayed Dad's dress shirts, including other garments with her mouth. She gracefully spat on each garment lying on el burro.

Ironing was always an all-nighter that seemed endless and agonizing. I hated ironing Dad's Sunday dress shirts— or anything, requiring special care and Mom's supervisory instructions.

There were two chores I hated most about being a girl: ironing and washing someone else's clothes.

The piles and piles of Dad and Mom's dress clothes on top of our clothes seemed endless. (Thank God Father worked in construction or else long sleeve dress shirts would have added more to the pile). As soon as Mom started setting up el burro—the ironing board—in what should have been half a dining room, but instead we used as a bedroom, I began my whining.

"Mom, but why do Paloma and I have to iron Dad's clothes?"

"¡Ay Sofia! You're so lazy!"

"It's just that I don't understand. I don't wear Dad's clothes. *Why us?*"

"Sofia, are you going to start? That mouth! ¡No seas tan preguntona! You always ask too many questions! You always talk back! That tongue of yours. *Where* did you learn those ways?"

When I nagged, my mother's facial gestures expressed her disappointment, and she turned her face away from me. *What had she done to deserve such a lazy daughter like myself?* With a cold bitter laugh, Mom responded, "Because he's your father," which I never understood.

Having to live in apartments also meant we needed to fight over laundromat visitation rights. If anybody left their clothing unattended and the dryer or washer cycle ended, Paloma had to spy to check if anyone was coming, and I'd quickly take out the clothing and place it on a folding table. I'd throw our clothes inside the washer or dryer, and then we'd run to our apartment; otherwise, we'd be washing and drying all day.

When we moved from Vista to San Marcos, that's when I noticed chores strategically favored the man in our family. For instance, we girls never carried out the trash like Dad—just heavy laundry baskets mounted with dirty clothes. To me, mowing the lawn didn't look difficult at all. It looked super easy and fun.

How to Mow the Long Green Grass
By Chofi Martinez
1) Check the lawn for Crucito's toys, Dad's nails,
and any other sharp objects, including rocks.

2) Add gasoline.

3) Turn the lawn mower's switch ON.

4) Press on the red jelly like button several times.

5) Pull the starter a couple of times.

6) Push the lawn mower with all your human strength.

If I could mow the lawn like a boy, at least I could be outside and listen to the singsong of finches, watch white butterflies flutter through the garden, greet and wave at neighbors passing by, and stare at the endless blue sky. But instead of Paloma and me mowing the lawn, Dad dropped us off at the laundromat on Mission Avenue next to the dairy to wash and fold everything from heavy king-sized Korean blankets to Dad's dirty and not so white underwear. Bras and underwear were the most embarrassing garments to dry, especially when red stained or not so new underwear fell to the ground, while we checked the clothes in the dryer. If an undergarment accidentally fell, it's not like we could ignore it and just leave it there when it was clear we were watching each other. For us, if someone looked at our bra or underwear, it was as if they were looking at our naked bodies. It was equivalent to watching feminine hygiene commercials in front of boys or even worse—Dad. Oh my God! ¡Trágame tierra!

Sometimes, when we barely had enough quarters and single dollar bills to spare in our imitation Ziploc bag, I'd window shop at the vending machine with its snacks and cigarettes then stare and admire the package labels with the bright oranges and mustardy yellows.

While we waited for the washer to end, we sat on the orange laundromat chairs (bolted to the ground in case anyone tried to steal them, I figured). My eyes wandered—at the graffiti, the announcements, the tile floor that needed a broom and a mop, the Spanish newspapers with the sexy ladies with their back to the readers wearing a two piece—a thong and high heels and the constant drop off and pick up of wives and daughters.

Swinging my feet back and forth out of boredom, I stared at the dryer's circular-glass door with the thick-black trim, where garments would slowly go round and round and round and round, painting a picture of a vanilla and chocolate ice cream swirl, which was like meditating in front of a TV screen. Another dryer gave form to a motley of colors from the palette of Matisse's bright yellows, blacks, oranges and greens Ms. Watson, my art teacher, had lectured on. And then, the dryer came to a full stop, and the colors—the burgundy red and thorny pink roses and the stoic lion—on heavy blankets took their true forms in need of folding.

Our Dream Home

Mom and Dad were always working for our dream house. In his early twenties, dressed in slacks and a tie, José Armando, our real estate agent, came to our apartment and talked to my parents about becoming homeowners. He sat patiently for what felt like hours translating endless paperwork. José Armando, Tijuana born with Sinaloa roots, grew up in Carlsbad, "Carlos Malos." He smelled like a professional, and the heaviness of his cologne and starchy clothes filled our small kitchen and living room long after he was gone. Our real estate agent felt like familia.

"Helena and Francisco, the contract states that if you complete all the renovations within a year, the bank will approve the loan. You can move in now, but the house is not in living conditions."

"But Jose Armando, I'm sure you've heard stories—*what if the gringo doesn't keep his promise?*" Mom asked our real estate agent.

"Helena, please trust me. Mr. Stoddard is a good man and will not back out of the deal because he signed the contract," José Armando assured Mom the owner would follow through. "You know Francisco more than I do. Your husband is going to make the house look like a palace—like your dream home. *Helena, the property even has a water well.* You can add the roses, calla lilies, and fruit trees you're looking for in a property. And, most importantly, you won't have to commute from Vista to San Marcos anymore."

Where Dad and Mom came from, waiting periods to build a house didn't exist; people didn't need permits to build a home made from adobe or blocks. In the U.S., however, my parents had to settle for a fixer-upper Dad could mend in no time with the help of family and friends.

When José Armando finally struck a deal with the owner, it took Dad a whole year to claim the house on 368 West San Marcos Boulevard as our own. After Dad came home from working construction all day, he'd work at home. Mom must have had sleepless nights when Father agreed to buy our first house. That's because Mother didn't see what Father saw. We would have a street number to ourselves, 368.

The first days at 368, Mom refused to eat in the kitchen, and how could she eat in *there*? How could her children eat in that *thing* Dad called kitchen? Yes, the house included a small stove, but cockroaches were baking their own feasts in the oven. Dad imagined a swing set for Crucito in the backyard's green lawn. But Mother had heard the neighbors walking by say the backyard turned into a swamp during the rainy seasons. Dad imagined a one-foot swallow lined with miniature plants that would keep the water moving to the large apartment complex next door. But Mom saw the swamp at our feet. Dad imagined the pantry and mom's new wooden cupboards. But Mom saw mice and cockroaches. Lots of cockroaches. Mom saw the faded dilapidated and peeling mint green paint. Dad saw a new wooden exterior and a fresh coat of paint.

Our new but old kitchen was infested with silky brown cockroaches—the thin kind that matched the plywood. Underneath the crawl space lived the critters, and at night, big roaches squeezed and welcomed themselves in through both the front and back door to drink water and eat crumbs. Paloma and I, in our superhero capes, made from black trash bags, became Las Cucaracha Warriors de la Noche and ran after the cucaracha bandits. We routinely turned off the lights, and then at about ten o'clockish, Mom turned on the kitchen lights, and Paloma and I charged at them. While they scattered everywhere, we all took our turns killing the horde of nightly visitors. The pest problem at 368 went away with endless nights of Raid attacks and hot water splashing. Paloma and I even conquered our cockroach phobia and squished cockroaches with our very own index fingers.

The master bedroom had seven layers of dusty carpets pancaked on top of each other. The wooden floor in our living room held itself together miraculously—we were always careful to wear shoes to prevent any splinters from pricking our bare feet.

When we finally settled into our new home, one Saturday morning Paloma and I still in our pajamas were arguing over who would have to sweep and mop before our parents got home from work when suddenly we found ourselves shoving and wrestling each other. And then with a big push, the unexpected happened. I flew through the wall.

"Oh my God, Chofi! Look what you did!"

"Look what *I* did? You pushed me, Mensa!"

Paloma and I had to reconcile immediately to cover up the crime scene.

When Dad got home later that afternoon and walked through the hallway to inspect our chores, he demanded an explanation, "*¿Y este pinche sofá? ¿Qué está haciendo aquí?*" Chanfles, we thought as our eyes placed the blame on each other. Dad gave us the mean Martinez Castillo stare with the white of his eyes showing that always worked, shook his head, and stormed out of the house because Dad knew he had to replace all the house's old plywood with new drywall.

Our idea of placing a love seat in front of the hole to cover it up didn't work. Our fear for our father's punishment turned into giggles and then uncontrollable laughter. Poking at each other's ribs and yelling at each other, "It's your fault!" and "No, it's your fault!" we almost peed our underwear. We laughed at the hole in the wall, the sofa that barely fit in the hallway that must have looked ridiculously out of place in our father's eyes, and at our new but old house facing the boulevard.

Strangers driving by honked or waved and gave Dad a thumbs up when he worked on our house on the weekends. We were living in Father's dream home, and we were happy. José Armando, our real estate agent, was right—Dad fixed our house, and Mother created her garden of dreams, where Dad and Mom planted hierbas santas. Orange, avocado, peach, cherimoya, guava, and purple fig trees. And native yellow-orange, deep-purple, and rose-colored milkweeds for our butterfly relatives who passed by and travelled south to Michoacán, our parents' homeland. One day we would follow them if Mom and Dad worked hard and saved enough money. One day.

The Guayaba Tree

In San Marcos, our backyard smelled like Idaho. The familiar smell of manure from the Hollandia Dairy on Mission Avenue lingered in our backyard. Months before the guava tree joined us at San Marcos Boulevard, Mom took free manure from the dairy for our garden and prepared the earth with water. Even if we already had a few trees, Dad and Mom talked about the trees and plants with special powers that would join our family. Next to the guayaba tree's new home, the apricot tree had already joined us, and now it was the guava tree's turn to step out of its black plastic container and to spread its roots and branches. At the end of the week with their Friday paycheck, Mom and Dad's eyes were set on an árbol de guayaba.

Right after work Dad drove us to the northside of San Marcos on the winding road to Los Arboleros, the tree growers' ranch on East Twin Oaks Valley Road, to buy the perfect tree for our backyard. As we approached a dirt road leading to the Santiago property, Don José in his sombrero and red and yellow Mexican bandana tied around his neck waved at us. At his side, two large Mexican wolfdogs with imposing orange eyes barked at us as we approached the nursery next to their house.

"Paloma and Chofi, be careful with Don Jose's dogs."

"Okay Ma," we answered in unison.

"Buenas tardes, Francisco and Helena. Don't worry, Señora Helena. My calupohs don't bite unless they smell evil. They scare off the coyotes that want to get into the chicken coop. Last week a red-shouldered hawk snatched one of my María's chickens in broad daylight." Don José's dogs, Yolotl and Yolotzin, sniffed our stiff bodies while I prayed to San Jorge Bendito: "San Jorge Bendito, amarra tus animalitos . . . ." Yolonzin sniffed and licked my hand. Thankfully, Don José's calupohs remembered us; we were in the clear. "If you need anything, holler at me. I'm going to water the foxtail palm trees on the other side."

At Don José and Doña María de la Luz Santiago's small ranch, Paloma and I were careful not to step on rattlesnakes. We walked through the rows of small trees in 15" containers and played with sticks next to a large flat boulder with smooth holes. I filled the holes with dead leaves and dirt and mixed it with a stick. "Paloma, let's ask Don Jose about the holes on this large boulder. How do you think these holes got here?" Paloma shrugged her shoulders and signaled with her head to get back. With the calupohs following us, we found Mom and Dad still deciding on a tree and a crimson red climbing rose bush.

"But Pancho, look how green the leaves look on this one!"

"Yes, Helena, but look at this one. It has a strong tree trunk."

"Pancho, this one has ripe fruit! Smell it, Pancho. With time, this one will be strong too."

"You're right, Helena. We can take the one you want. Let's pay Don Jose and get going before it gets too dark, so we can plant our tree today."

"Yes, Pancho, it's a full moon!"

"Paloma and Chofi, I'm glad you're both back. Go look for Don Jose, and tell him we're ready to pay."

Paloma and I ran to look for Don José. On our way to find him, I remembered we needed to ask him about the holes on the boulder.

"Hola Don Jose. My mom and dad are ready to pay."

"Let's go then."

"Don Jose, we have a question for you. We saw a big flat rock on your property, and we're wondering how the holes got there."

Don José cleaned his sweat with his bandana and gave us a pensive look.

"Those holes. Well, Chofi, as you may know, this land you see here from Oceanside all the way to Palomar Mountain and beyond was inhabited by Native people. Women sat and pounded acorns on metates like the one you saw and made soup and other foods. You can only imagine how many years it took for those indentations to leave their mark and to withstand time. Those women, Chofi and Paloma, left their mark."

"Oh, wow, Don Jose. That's why the road is called Twin Oaks Valley Road? It's a reference to Native people's trees, who lived in this area?"

"Yes, Chofi and Paloma. Native people still live on these lands—in Escondido, San Marcos, Valley Center, Fallbrook, Pala, and Pauma Valley and beyond. Ask your U.S. history teacher about the people who inhabited these lands. I'm sure they can tell you more."

"Thank you, Don Jose. I'll ask."

Dad and Mom paid Don José, and off we went to plant our

guayaba tree. With our guava tree sticking out of the window in the Monte Carlo and lying on Paloma, Crucito, and me in the back seat, Mom was all smiles and kept glancing back.

"Pancho, please drive slowly and turn on your emergency lights. Children, hold onto our tree carefully."

"Don't worry Helena. Two more stop lights, and we're almost home."

Dad agreed to Mom's pick because he knew she loved guayabas—all kinds. This time they chose the one with the two guayabas with pink insides, which wasn't too sweet and just about my height. I preferred the bigger trees at Los Arboleros. Why couldn't we get bigger trees? Mom and Dad always chose the smaller trees because those were the ones we could afford, and plus we didn't have a truck like our neighbor Don Cipriano's, but maybe we could borrow it next time.

As soon as we arrived home, Dad cut the container down the middle with a switchblade, and Mom pushed the shovel down with her right foot and split the earth.

"¡Ay, ay! ¡Ay Pancho! Be careful with the tree's roots. Here, grab the shovel. Let me hold onto the arbolito."

Dad dug the hole, exposing the dark brown of the earth as two pink worms shied away from the light.

"Dad, can Crucito and me get the worms, *pleaseee*?"

"Hurry up Chofi and Cruz. Go ahead. Your mom and I want to plant the tree today."

"Okay, Apá!"

While I carefully took the worms from their home, Mom held the guava tree as if she held a wounded soldier and whispered to the tree, "Arbolito, don't worry. You're going to be safe here. I'm going to water you when you get thirsty and take care of you—we all will."

"Pancho, one day we're going to make agua de guayaba."

"Sí, Helena, we're going to make guayabate like the one my mom used to make. It was so good!"

"I bet it was, Pancho. To prevent a bad cough, my mom used to give us guava tea to fight off the flu."

"Helena, did you know guava leaves are also good for hangovers?"

"Ay Pancho. ¿Qué cosas dices? Let's get this tree planted."

From the dried-up manure pile, Dad mixed the native soil and compost and pulled the weeds. As Mom placed the root-ball above the hole, they both looked for the guava tree's face and centered the tree on top of the hole. With the shovel, Dad poured the dirt around the tree. Mom took the shovel from Dad and pounded softly on the dirt surrounding the guava tree, making sure they left the edge below the surface.

Next to the apricot tree with a woody surface, the small guava tree with tough dark green leaves would be heavy with fruit one day for our family, our neighbors, and friends. Dad went looking for a canopy for the young guava tree to protect her from winter's threatening frostbite, and mom stood in the garden, admiring our new family member.

It was time to return the worms to the earth; they were so tender but so strong. I made a little hole with my hand, placed the worms inside, said thank you to the worms, and covered them with dirt. The guayaba tree would make a perfect home.

Las Muy Muy

At our new school, San Marcos Elementary, no more than a hundred feet away from our house on West San Marcos Boulevard, we were las que se creían muy muy, the ones who thought they were *all that*. Not because we were spoiled but because we only spoke English at school. Ironically, the kids at our new school didn't know we were coming from Vista's Santa Fe Elementary—an English only school.

"Ay sí. Se creen muy muy," said Yenny with her imposing short stature as she dug her little white tennis shoe on the playground's black asphalt and pushed her small frame forward with her arms crossed. At school, the voices echoed through the hallways as we walked by.

"They only want to speak *English*."

"Look at *them*. They only speak *English*."

"Se creen muy muy."

"Sefe crefen mufuy mufuy."

But, because Mrs. Clifton, our teacher, talked privately to Yenny and the girls who taunted us most and explained why we only spoke English at school, the bullying stopped.

Many of the students at San Marcos Elementary had been born here, but they didn't speak English. We, the Martinez sisters, had become miniature robots with ON and OFF switches, programmed to only speak English at school and Spanish at home even when Dad wasn't around.

Father had made it very clear we would only be speaking Spanish at home. "Aquí—en esta pinche casa—sólo se habla español," he would say as his throat tightened and turned rooster red. And our Mexican father was no joke, for someone like my father who upheld Mexican standards, since it would be embarrassing for a Mexican-born to raise children who didn't speak Spanish. Or God forbid Mexican parents raise a child with a pocho accent who spoke Spanglish or a child who didn't speak Spanish at all.

One Christmas the school sent us home with a Christmas gift booklet. If our class sold the most items, we would get an ice cream party as a reward. And because I wanted to win an ice cream treat, I walked on East Los Angeles Street, next to our apartment complex, selling what my parents couldn't afford. I stood at a door on East Indian Rock Street feeling overwhelmed by the flood of questions and answered, "I don't speak Spanish."

When those words came out of my mouth, I didn't know where they had come from. What I did know is Dad would never find out about this incident. Never never. Nunca nunca.

The Belt

Once a month, Mom's brother and Dad's construction friends came over to demolish walls and to hammer away at our new but old house that was falling apart inside, which meant a carne asada and the cousins coming over from faraway places. Except a minor inconvenience didn't allow the families to have fun together, a family feud. Paloma and I were stuck in a tug of war—torn between the Ramirez cousins on mom's side of the family.

During one of those family gatherings, Sandra, Poncho's little sister, feeding off Aunt Carlota's manipulation, didn't want to play with the group. And Paloma and I weren't willing to stop talking to the cousins who were visiting all the way from Santa Ana. The fun ended when Aunt Carlota didn't see us playing with Sandra. Our aunt went over to talk to Uncle David and demanded we include her. So our uncle came over to our play area next to the Canary palm's shade to talk to us.

"Sofia, why aren't you playing with your cousin, Sandra?"

"Uncle David, we've already asked Sandra to play with us. *She* doesn't want to play with all of us."

"Sofia, you need to play with her too."

"But Uncle David, we already asked her."

"Do you want me to tell your father you're not including Sandra?"

"*Tell him.*"

What happened next, I didn't see coming.

Within less than five minutes of Uncle David leaving, Dad came over to our play area and dragged me by the arm to my room—a corner of a boxing ring. The sound of his steel buckle unjawing prepared me for the belt. By the second whip, like a heavy weight striking a light weight, I fell to the ground, bracing myself and swaying to the left and then to the right every time the leather belt whipped my body.

Like a fixed match, I took all the blows. There was no referee to stop him. When Father finished whipping me, sobs filled my chest. My swollen eyes closed shut, and my tongue turned inward. Father didn't believe in hitting children, but when Uncle David confronted him about his daughter talking back to him, everything changed. I crossed the invisible line that in my eyes deserved crossing. That was the first time Father hit me like that because some words, I learned—coming from a girl—had consequences. So began the taming of the hocicona in me.

San Marcos, Twelve

It was the day after April Fool's Day, Thursday, April 2, 1987, at about 9:17 AM.

It felt like waiting for long awaited mail, and then when you finally checked your mailbox, the envelope in your hands was addressed to someone else who no longer lived there.

What looked like a tiny drop of fruit-punch mix dissolving in a crystal-clear pitcher of water grew red octopus legs and uncurled from the inner crevice of two enormous rocks. The problem was that I wasn't sure if the long-awaited mail was mine or not because I thought it was another girl's mail. For the first time, I hadn't checked the toilet before sitting down.

A few months prior both Mom and Dad had objected to either Paloma or me attending sex education classes. There were no warnings. We didn't trick Dad or Mom into signing that form. We checked the NO box for them. Our parents couldn't read books, but they sure were good at reading us.

Friday. 7:46 AM. That morning I woke up late to what the boys called a wet dream except mine was a deep red chocolate wet dream, but I was living the dream. It was the color of mole—so dark—hand soap couldn't remove the manchas from my favorite pair of turquoise-colored pajamas. With fourteen minutes before the bell rang for school to start, I did my best to hide the evidence. I didn't tell anyone—not even Paloma.

7:48 AM. In an instant replay, as I stared at my pajamas, I realized that that tiny red octopus I had seen in the toilet the day before *had been mine*. YES, MINE! That drop of blood was like a scene in *Clash of the Titans* where Perseus waves Medusa's head underwater at the sea monster, and her snake hair hisses and sways in slow motion like seaweed underwater. Except the little red drop with tentacles hadn't been scary at all.

4:40 PM. Mother came home from Spanjan. She had never talked to us about sanitary pads, tampons, or "burros," d o n k e y s, as the girls at San Marcos Elementary called them. Mother found out about my first period because our babysitter told her. Manchas were like mole—they told stories without words.

6:38 PM. Later that evening with the full moon peering through the kitchen window, I sat at the dinner table and Dad said in an angry tone, "Helena, didn't you tell this girl she can't eat avocados? And that she can't try out for track either!" My eyes widened as I stared at the slice of green avocado in front of me. Mother had betrayed me.

Dad knew?

An avocado?

What did avocados have to do with my regla?

WHAT? I couldn't run out for track anymore because of my period?

I was stuck with my imagination, wondering about my period, avocados, and a ruler. Aguacates, cacahuates, tanates—it took me a few years to figure out Dad's riddle that made perfect sense when I looked up the word avocado in the bible-thin pages of my thick *Webster's Dictionary*. With my index finger on the word avocado—ahuacatl—I laughed like Medusa or was it Coatlicue because my period was a sign everything was working and ticking in my sixth-grade girl's body.

Dad had been afraid I'd get near avocados, *and I would be too.*

Aguacates—they were so soft, mushy, and tender and made periods go away, according to my Mexican father, Francisco Martinez Castillo.

And he was right.

The Boy Who Moved Far, Far Away

"Chiquitita sabes muy bien
Que las penas vienen y van y desaparecen
Otra vez vas a bailar y serás feliz
Como las flores que florecen"
                                        —ABBA, "Chiquitita"

At our freshly painted creamy yellow house with brick red colored trim at 368 San Marcos Boulevard, a torrent of salty tears blurred my vision and flooded my heart. When the boy who I had kept a thirty-six-inch distance between us told me he had to move away, my heart got as big as a seedy watermelon growing inside my chest exponentially like a fast forward in time. And its seeds were tiny tears waiting to burst in my big screaming red heart.

Eduardo, this was the same boy, who I didn't allow to hold my sweaty left hand out of embarrassment. Eduardo Zapata, the brown Mexicali boy, whose clothes fit me perfectly for cross dressing day—the boy who stopped the gossip about me from spreading at school.

Eduardo.

When he told me the news about him moving away *over the telephone*, I couldn't breathe. I couldn't see. As much as I told my body to breathe—to calm down—that everything would

65

be okay, I couldn't. I did try, but it felt like I had a green guava stuck in my throat, suffocating the wailing inside. *What could I say?* I wasn't a novela type of girl—I had no practice. Our mother was not like that either. I couldn't cover my eyes and scream, "¡Eduardo Zapata! *How could you do this to me? I hate you! I will never forgive you!*"

When we hung up the phone, I sat on the back porch with a pail of tears at my feet for a cholo boy who would be moving far, far away to a city called Escondido—hidden—away from me, forever and ever. I stared at the backyard at the empty swings set, swaying back and forth, as I tried making sense of the blur before me when a light tap on my right shoulder interrupted my tears. Startled, I gathered myself and looked around. It wasn't Crucito or Paloma. Sitting on the back porch, I could feel the pounding of my head, my big, fat heart made of red pulp and my cold, empty hands. My heart ached again like Poe in a world looking "for a love that was more than love."

When my parents got home from work, I couldn't tell them about the guava stuck in my throat or the tap on my shoulder because I wasn't allowed to have a boyfriend, and Mom and Dad would find out about my secret boyfriend, E d u a r d o, who would no longer be my boyfriend no more. Never never again for ever and ever.

"Helena, what's wrong with Chofi? Did you see her eyes? Has she been crying?"

"Pancho, creo que anda en su luna. Déjala en paz. Le duele su pansita. Le voy hacer un tecito de hierbabuena para que se le quite el dolor."

La Migra Chasing My Mind

It always happened. We always fell for the same joke. On our way to school, one of the girls in the pack would scream, "¡La Migra!" And sure enough, Paloma and I would start running—for a few seconds—until we both realized we had been born here in the United States. Our birth certificates stated clearly, "Caucasian." Not Hispanic. The irony is we didn't identify as either.

Our girlfriends laughed—drowned in laughter—as we walked past apartment complex after apartment complex and finally crossed the train tracks onto Mission Avenue to San Marcos Junior High School. After a few minutes of mocking us, Arianna would catch her breath and ask, "*Why do you run?*" We would stare at each other and shrug our shoulders.

"We run for the same reasons you do."

"*But both of you were born here.*"

It took us many years to understand why we ran. Our parents didn't run. I recollected the time when La Migra swung by the Ritz Theatre on Grand Avenue and Broadway Street in Downtown Escondido. La Migra would sometimes catch paisanos after the last show like the time Uncle David's family and our family saw a group of church acquaintances—a family of little brown Mexicans shorter than my father, being followed and pulled over by immigration officials. Uncle David tried to swerve in front of La Migra. But it was too late. We never saw them again. Because in the eyes of La Migra, some people were easier to catch than others.

As a matter of fact, I realized I had never seen anyone run from La Migra, but the stories I heard were enough to make me fear the men in green, Los Limones. They were sour business. There was the story of one of my uncles living in L.A., who at the sight of the mailman, panicked and ran for fear of being caught. I imagined Uncle Monico (that was his paper name) running for his life as the postman went on his daily rendez-vous delivering mail.

Arianna's "*Why do you run?*" wasn't so easy to explain.

Put Your Hands over Your Head

When it wasn't La Migra chasing our mind, it was La Chota. That day we had gone on a walk with Uncle David when I recognized a familiar smell.

"Ay! It smells like marijuana."

"*Sofía Martinez, how do you know what marijuana smells like?*" Uncle David demanded an explanation.

"Uncle, one day our babysitter, Angela, took us to the park, and she said, 'Esos gringos van bien marijuanos.' That's how I remember the smell of marijuana. *I swear.*"

The tires of a beat-up Nova shrieked as two gringos turned the corner on Indian Rock Street and East Los Angeles Street, and a distinct scent trailed behind them and into my memory of smells.

When my godmother Cleo and her family moved in with us because there were too many earthquakes in northern Alta California, she went on walks after work to calm her nerves. One day, by the freeway exit on San Marcos Boulevard, she found a mysterious looking plant in a small pot. She picked up the plant and had to find a home for the healthy-looking plantita, sitting abandoned on the side of the road. And mom's medicine garden came to Madrina Cleo's mind, so when she got home, she told everyone about her new-found plant, whose leaves were a deep green and looked like a star fish's arms with purple flowers.

"¡Ay Mija! Look at my little green plantita. ¡Está bien bonita!" It was a different type of green though—not like Mom's glossy indoor plants. As soon as Paloma looked at the pot, she panicked and screamed, "Tía Cleo, that's MARIJUANA!"

At first, my godmother, reluctant to get rid of her little green finding, pulled the small pot away from Paloma.

"Marijuana? Are you sure, Mija?"

"Yes, Tía Cleo! Rudy 'El Trucha,' our neighbor across the street on Johnston Lane, is serving life for selling five pounds of marijuana to an undercover cop!"

"¡Ay Dios mío, Mija!" my godmother screamed.

Cruz and the cousins ran around the backyard not knowing what to do. I imagined my madrina being followed by a helicopter, and any minute a loudspeaker would blare, "Put the plant down! I repeat put the plant down! Everyone put your hands over your head. Get down on your knees! You're all under arrest!" And for sure we'd lose our house after all of Dad and Mom's hard work.

Paloma was right. In the 80s, people like El Trucha got locked up and did some serious prison time for a little defenseless green plantita, hiding in Mom's garden of dreams, that grew out of the earth and talked to Black and Brown folk—and White folk too. Pa' que se hacían.

Make Believe

Before sleep time, without hallucinogens, Mother was good at a game she invented herself—Make Believe. Sometimes she would ask Paloma and me to imagine we had lots of money and ask, "What would you do with a million dollars?" This time Mom started with, "Let's make believe we're lost, and we don't know where we're at."

While awake, it was difficult to imagine any other place because we were on Rancho Santa Fe Road in our family car about seven miles away from our home. On the radio, Dad played La Poderosa 109, and every passing building looked so familiar but only from the outside—Miller's Outpost, Mc-Donald's, and the Bowl Weevil, places none of which we were frequent customers at. Our imagination took us to cities like Los Ángeles, Mexicali, and Tijuana on our three-day weekends, and here was Mom asking us to make believe a place we could only imagine by reading books and watching movies.

Straight faced, Dad pulled into the Miller's Outpost parking lot and commanded, "Paloma, go ask that woman, wearing a fedora hat, where we're at." Paloma, Cruz, and I in the back seat stared at each other with facial gestures signaling our confusion. *Why was Dad asking such a bizarre request?* Even Mom looked confused. Dad told Mom, sitting next to him in the passenger's seat, "*Helena*, I thought you said we were playing

Make Believe." We all started laughing with our mouths wide open with our campanitas showing like when the doctor stuck a Popsicle-looking-stick in our mouths.

Inside our Chevrolet, the color of sweet caramel, our laughs were like Christmas lights. My sister's laugh, my brother's and my laugh were syncopated Christmas lights. Green. Red. Yellow. Then, yellow, red and green. Dad and Mom's laughs were synchronized peaceful blue and white lights because they had been together for a long time. By now we were eastbound on Highway 78 in Mother's time traveler machine, El Monte Carlo, on our way to Make Believe because we were a family of dream makers, imagining dream worlds.

Playing with Fire

When Mom and Dad didn't work on Saturdays, we left on Friday evenings in our time traveler to desert lands Dad's family called home. In Mexicali, the scorching sun picked at our skin all day, and at night, the warm desert wind smothered our faces. The older cousins and their friends snuck away behind the shrubs and kissed in the dark while the younger ones played with a full tank of gasoline. Cousin Mundo poured gasoline on the dry, barren outskirts of his father's land, and then one of his friends dropped the match. When cousin Lupita saw the fire's long fingers reach for us, she yapped, "Vámonos de aquí porque allí viene el Diablo en chinga." As Lupita pulled me away from the flames, Beto, Tía Alicia and Uncle Carlos's son, stood staring at the ground engulfed in flames while the others pranced around the fire.

Away from home, we stayed up past our bedtime as our eyes glistened in the dark, marveling at bonfires and a blanket of stars high above in the darkest of skies. Out in the open, those were the wild nights, where the Martinez cousins banded together and yelped like wild coyotes. Dad's brothers and sisters drank, sang, and howled the night away inside the cool brick walls of Uncle Reymundo's flat-roof home with spirits and guitars strumming rancheras.

Dad always had his guard up for girls, including at family gatherings, even if they weren't his own daughters.

"Mundo, have you seen your daughter?"

"Isn't she with all the kids?"

"No, Mundo. I saw Maria with one of the chavalos behind the arrowweeds. Carnal, at her age she shouldn't be experimenting."

"Little brother, why don't you mind your own business? Nothing is going to happen to the plebes. I have my family to take care of. And you have your own. Besides, do you think your daughters are going to be yours forever?"

"No—but I want my girls to go to college and not to roll around with the first chavalo they see."

"*College? Seriously Carnal? Paloma and Sofia go to college?* Where do you get your crazy ideas from? College is not for us. Did you already forget what happened to our Primo Miguel? College is impossible Carnal—*you and Helena don't even know how to read.* You haven't even saved enough money to visit Michoacán. With what money are you going to send the girls off to college?"

"Really Carnal? *You're going to bring up our Primo Miguel right now? Have some respect—let spirits rest.* That happened in Mexico City in 1968. We're talking about your Maria. Mundo, we haven't even celebrated Maria's quinceañera yet."

"Pancheras, stop that superstition. Nothing is going to happen. What the girls need to learn is to live their own lives. *Did you already forget the day when you and Chencha went missing for hours—and you and her finally came down the hill?* You had the whole town of Los Reyes, especially Mom and Chencha's mom, worried and looking for her."

"But Reymundo—do you want the same thing that happened to you to happen to your Maria?"

"Chale Carnal. You come all the way to Chicali to see me, and this is what you want to talk about? My Maria and college? She's here. Come on take another tequila shot."

Paper Boys Were a Sin

Dad mistrusted boys even the dead ones. Ever since we could remember, Dad told us he would never give our hand in marriage or attend our wedding. Instead, Dad wanted us to go to school and get educated. I felt sorry for Paloma because she did want a big fancy wedding and get married in a big fluffy puffy white dress, carrying a bouquet of flowers down the aisle. Well, at least Paloma didn't want to wear white shiny high heels; instead, she wanted to wear white cowboy boots. I, on the other hand, couldn't picture myself in a wedding dress—as much as I tried.

Dad even mistrusted boys on posters. With growls and roars, he raided our room and tore all the boy posters off our bedroom walls and stomped on the Menudo boys. He turned into The Incredible Hulk but more like The Incredible Red. Without saying a word and his veins popping out from his neck, Dad roared and shredded every filament of testosterone that could corrupt us, his daughters. After Dad finished destroying our heartthrobs plastered on our bedroom's walls, he fired out of our room and slammed the door behind him.

Dad missed my Elvis Presley's Jailhouse Rock poster clinging to the door. After Dad left, in the middle of the room, I stood staring at Elvis gyrating his hips. Strumming my imaginary guitar, I smiled and giggled inside like Mona Lisa and winked my left eye at Elvis. And he returned my wink. I took out my strawberry ChapStick, moisturized my dry lips, and puckered my lips at Elvis.

Los Chores

At school or anywhere we went, Mom insisted we always wear shorts—chores—underneath our dresses and skirts because *somebody* would see us. And, of course, to our mother it made perfect sense. On the playground, if we got on the swings or the monkey bars wearing shorts, the boys couldn't look at our calzones. Just in case we fell, passersby would only see our chores not the underwear underneath our skirts.

At San Marcos Junior High School inside the girl's locker room, it embarrassed us to have to undress publicly even if we were in a room full of girls. We overused the "I have to pee really bad" excuse to hide and change in the bathroom stalls quickly, and it upset the girls who were waiting in line to really use the toilet.

Paloma full-heartedly abided by our mother's rules and took it to the next level—high school. At San Marcos High School, under no circumstances would we ever get caught **NAKED** in the girl's locker room.

What would our mother say?

God forbid we showered at school like the hueras—not even after sweating profusely after running the mile. Not even after bench pressing with teenage boys. No way. Never never.

Going into her senior year, Paloma still wore a pair of chores underneath her dress. Mom trained my sister well. Not me—shorts underneath my dresses, including underwear, were annoying and uncomfortable to wear.

The Leg

"Mija, if a man touches your leg, it's not that he loves you. It's that he wants to fuck you," Father warned me in a convincing tone. Feeling awkward listening to his one-minute sex education lecture on our way to Joey's Tacos, I sat in our old Monte Carlo's passenger's seat because Mom too proper and religious for this kind of talk would have nothing to do with such a vulgar topic.

His words meant if a chavalo touched my knee and tried going to other places—he was nothing but a player. And that male behavior, I learned was below my standards, and I should despise.

I learned to read men. It was easy. If guys looked a little too long elsewhere but my face, I knew what was crossing their mind. So, when boys with deep, throaty voices and long rico suave finger gestures came my way, I ran, turned the block and blew goodbye kisses. Once boys got too close to my knee, like a recurrent nightmare that didn't go away, I'd hear my father's haunting words echo: "*It's not that he loves you; it's that he wants to fuck you. It's not that he loves you . . . Mija, no es que te quiera; es que te quiere chingar.*"

". . . Good luck, Sofia"

My palms sweat and my throat locked when family, friends, and strangers asked me the college question.

I did and didn't know the answer.

Mom and Dad had planted in us the seed that, yes indeed, we were going to college, and they told everyone: "Nuestras hijas, Paloma y Sofia, van a ir al colegio."

But my K-12 teachers and counselors had never mentioned college. How did one go to college? Was college like high school?

"So, what are you doing after high school?" circled and circled my mind. I had the answer but didn't know if anybody would believe me. I wanted to go to college, so one day I could be a kindergarten teacher who didn't place children in a corner of the classroom for speaking Spanish in school nor punish children for not knowing how to write their name.

While catching a ride to work with Alex—because Dad had had too many beers—I started panicking just thinking about what I would answer if he asked *the question*. Alex, who lived a block away, attended the local community college's police academy and wanted to be a chota, asked me *THE QUESTION* I dreaded being asked because I didn't know if I was going to go to college like Dad assured.

I was glad it would only be a ten-minute ride to Joey's Tacos on East San Marcos Boulevard because that meant he'd do most of the talking. Alex made college sound so easy. At work, "Hello. Welcome to Joey's Tacos. Would you like to try our Street Taco, seasoned carne asada, minced onions, and secret sauce on a hot corn tortilla?" was much easier to repeat than having to answer, "*So what are you doing after high school?*"

Since responding to that question was so difficult for me to answer, I started practicing in my mind and repeating, "*I'm going to college. I'm going to college. I'm going to college,*" in front of the mirror, so I could be ready to answer the question with confidence the next time someone asked me.

The day Alex dropped me off right before our lunch rush at work—of all places—Roberto, my manager at Joey's Tacos, asked, "So, Sofia, what are you doing after high school?" I was ready to answer the question and surprised myself when the words escaped my mouth effortlessly and loudly, "*I'm going to college.*"

I had finally forced my tongue to speak and believe in my parents' dream for Paloma, Crucito, and me. And my tongue followed my mind's orders! My manager, a high school dropout now twenty-two-years old, chuckled and scoffed, "Yeah—right. *Good luck, Sofia.*"

No one believed us, besides our parents, we were going to college.

BUT WHY?

A Doorway of Her Own

At work, she was the girl with the long and beautiful yellow hair. Her sister bleached her hair, and her mother did too. Blanca's skin was Cover Girl soft and her lips were Little Red Riding Hood red. That Blanca was a good girl—perfect—in their eyes. In the eyes of many, she was perfect—good grades, organized, punctual and most importantly, hardworking and blanquita. She was the daughter of strict religious parents—stricter than my parents, who also attended St. Mark's Catholic Church.

At Joey's Tacos, where we worked together after school, Blanca was so smart and fast she got promoted to spreading precooked ground beef from plastic bags on flour tortillas (that tasted different—not like the ones we ate at home). Sometimes, I hopped on the production line, where little cockroaches crawled out of the steam table, and of course, it made sense even to a cockroach to run away from hot steam. It felt awkward to prepare food with a little brigade of baby cockroaches, squeezing out of the crevices of hot stainless steel. So, I'd go to the office and get tape—the clear type—to stop the single-file cockroach march.

At the end of our lunch rush with customers out of the door dancing to "Hot. Hot. Hot. It's getting hot, hot, hot," I stripped off my invention—the Clear Cockroach Stopper— with no dirty messes or traces. When I stared at those little cucarachitas, I was glad I couldn't hear their screams.

No one said anything.

No one said Blanca would crawl out of her bedroom window into the night while her father slept. Her mother was the type who woke up in the middle of the night to check up on her children. But Blanca outsmarted her own mother; she placed pillows underneath her blankets. No one noticed, except her accomplice—her sister.

Blanca wanted to be free, but she was underage and still living at home. Out into the dark night, Blanca disappeared on San Marcos Boulevard until one early dawn there was a power outage where the gringo lived, and the alarm clock didn't wake them up as usual. By then, it was too late. She was pregnant, turning eighteen in a few weeks, and the gringo wanted nothing to do with her. And an abortion would never be an option for Blanquita and her parents.

The Dream Story

"Dad, tell us one of your stories," Paloma pleaded.

"A story? Which one do you want to hear?"

"Chofi, you pick a story this time. I picked last time."

"Your dream story—the one about you not knowing how to write your name."

"The dream story? That one? *Why that one?*"

"I don't know."

"Sofia, you always pick the sad stories. Okey pues, aquí va. I was standing at a Check Cashing place with a check fumbling through my hands when I asked a stranger, who looked like a paisano, if he could sign my check. 'Me puedes firmar mi cheque?' I asked him as he walked away and fanned green dollar bills through his fingers. He looked at me as if he'd never witnessed anything stupider than someone like me unable to claim his own sweat. Refusing to sign my check, the man told me, 'A cómo eres pendejo. You don't even know how to sign your own check.'" Dad cleared his throat and held back tears. "That day I swore one day my children would go to school, so no one would humiliate them for not knowing how to sign their name. And I will keep my promise because I come from an oral tradition, where written words on a paper mean nothing and will not alter my destiny. Like those stranger's words stepped on me, my words can be earsplitting, and my tongue can lash out too. Al papel con la lluvia se le caen las letras; a mi palabra no. My children—Paloma, Sofia, and Cruz—you will be college educated—not to make you better people, but instead so you can unriddle the world you were born into. So one day you can stand your ground firmes mis hijas y hijo aquí en Alta California or anywhere in the world."

Consumed with silence, Paloma, Crucito, and I took in Dad's words. We couldn't imagine how any person could humiliate and step on someone for not knowing how to write their name because those words stay with a person forever. That was the power of my father's tongue, telling stories and not being afraid to speak the truth. Even if Dad hadn't gone to school, he didn't stay quiet; he asked questions. In my father's dream, we have food, words, and numbers, so one day we don't have to sign a check with a humble X.

Stories Tía Alicia Told Us

He left Michoacán, the place where a hungry child gnawed the sweetest strips of sugarcane and a desperate man poured 100% ethanol down his throat to make the memory of his children go away, and in his desperation, he flew north. With children younger than himself dying of malnutrition, Panchito, my little brother, ate rolled corn tortillas sprinkled with salt and drank diluted evaporated milk to silence his hunger and muffle the sounds of a painful empty stomach.

In those days, a sliced pig would never go to waste because meat was a once a year squeal for those who could afford a pig. Poor people like us ate everything from soft brain, gummy eyes, chewy tripe, and a juicy tongue. And if the salsa was just right—it was the perfect taco eaters' high, because when the chiles and salt kicked in, taco lovers forgot their hunger for just a little bit.

Mijas, from Michoacán to Mexicali, your father followed his dream—in search of better tomorrows. He worked hard and earned his own money. He was street taco smart and learned street taco fast because the language of tacos tamed a Mexican tongue. Once in Mexicali, one of the earth's hottest comales, he made the best tacos de cabeza a teenage boy could make with a rented food cart and for himself five extra pounds of meat under the cart for him to sell. Your father made tacos packed with cebollita and cilantro that made passersby swallow them in two bites. His butcher knife danced "El jarabe tapatío" on a slab of meat, which soon looked like minced meat with the last remache tap, tap, tap. A wooden platform shook with taca tataca tataca sounds luring passersby for their taste of a taco tatataco.

Así fue, Mijas. The money your father earned he sent to our parents, your grandparents, who live in Los Reyes, Michoacán. I bet my brother, Pancho, and my cuñada, Helena, have told you all about your Abuelitos.

"Lo bonito no te quita lo pendejo . . ."

Reymundo "Mundo" Martinez Castillo. His wedding picture hung from our living room wall next to the life size replica of la Virgen de Guadalupe. Much to his misfortune, he was handsome. Uncle Mundo looked like El Mariachi.

And because Uncle Mundo, Dad's older brother, had a handsome face, he wasn't afraid of anything living or dead, and that was his downfall. That's what landed him in an ambulance on his way to the ER at 2:35 AM on an early Wednesday morning.

Before Uncle Mundo moved to Mexicali, he was a regular at El Camino, one of the local bars in Burbank, where he started with two tequila shots to warm up the body that was already caliente. With a cigarette in his mouth blowing smoke rings like a real chingón and gold fangs glimmering, he impressed the ladies, who sat on bar stools with their breasts popping out and skimpy skirts kicking their crossed legs in his direction. He entertained women who flipped their hair to get his attention with his large piercing brown eyes and his bullshit stories. Without a guitar to entice the ladies, his words were like honey. Because his voice strung hearts, women stuck like flies and bees, and they weren't going anywhere without a little bit of Mundo's touch.

Uncle Mundo's presence was dangerous among men. Because if he wanted and when he wanted, Mundo could easily borrow a stranger's lady friend like the day they waited for him outside and gunned him down as he left El Camino. Five bullets and one bullet graze left him with his left arm in a permanent position as if he was carrying a gun close to his rib cage.

That's what happened to pretty people. They thought they were invincible—immune to danger like Icarus. But because they had pretty faces, they grew enormous wings. And then blinded by their hubris, they flew high and plummeted down, spiraling out of control.

One day, when I have children, sobrinas and sobrinos of my own, I will tell them, "Lo bonito no te quita lo pendejo, so don't rely on your pretty looks like your Uncle Reymundo. Think. *Haven't you heard what happened to the model Viva Bellagio?* How many times has her pretty face and ass landed in jail? Piensa, Mija. Piensa, Mijo."

The Music's Heartbeat

It didn't matter where my father's family lived—on this or on the other side of the border. Dad's big family heard music in the tap of the rain, in the cockle-doodle-doo of a rooster, and the blow of a hammer. At family parties, Tío Juan, no longer able bodied and with two weak knees, now danced with his mouth. At parties, his tongue frolicked impatiently as if he were feeling the music's heartbeat with his prancing tongue. Captivated by Tío Juan's moves, I imagined he felt the music with his tongue.

On the dance floor, Uncle Mundo, flying through guests' feet, made him—at forty-seven—the star of the dance floor as he transformed into a flying iguana. "Uy, uy, uy que iguana tan fea. Miren cómo se menea. Uy, uy, uy que iguana tan loca. Miren cómo abre la boca. Uy, uy, uy que se sube al palo. Uy, uy, uy que ya se subió. Uy, uy, uy que busca su cueva." With his head cocked, red mustache twitching, swaying and jumping across the dance floor with the ease of a reptile, Uncle Mundo's body spearheaded to women's feet as they shooed him away with their rebozos.

Tía Alicia with her body shaped like a butternut squash danced like an enchanted cobra. Gracefully, to the music's rhythms, our aunt swayed her hips side to side to cumbias as she sang and danced to "La pollera colora."

"Ay, al sonar los tambores

Esta negra se amaña

Al sonar de la caña

Van brindando sus amores."

Men, young and old, stood in line mesmerized like rabbits by the young snake woman. And they waited their turn for a slow dance in hopes of entangling their fingers in Alicia's long wavy dark brown hair.

Dad told me his youngest brother, Uncle Román, used to dance too—on a rope. The circus swept him away. Gracefully, he sped across the rope dancing to the violin's sweet, syncopated sounds of "El jarabe tapatío." Years later, Abuelita Chucha missed her Romancito so much her heart ached, so she called her son back. My abuelita summoned the winds. She lay facing down on a crossroad and hollered at the earth. "*Romaaannnn! Romaaannnn! Romaaannnncitoooo! My son—return!*" so la tierra and los vientos would return her Romancito back to her.

And the Earth's winds did listen to Abuelita Chucha and heard her calling. That's why Uncle Roman returned home to my grandmother's arms. One day, while feeding a hungry lion, the beast clawed him, and my uncle almost lost his right leg. From miles and miles away, Uncle Roman heard the music of his mother's voice in the wind, and that's why he returned to Michoacán.

Alicia in the Company of Men

"La cruz no pesa lo que cala.
Son los filos. Cariño santo.
Cariño santo . . ."
—Lucha Villa, "Bala perdida"

As well as telling stories and dancing, Tía Alicia also sang her grief away after her hair got entangled in sadness. Without a guitar to accompany her singing, when Tía Alicia's vocal cords struck, she echoed a block away. At family gatherings, her brava voice filled our backyard in San Marcos and brought out the mariachi howl in us. In between songs with thunder and lightning coming from her throat, Tía Alicia, father's sister, hollered: "¡Y muévanse cabrones, porque si no, no empieza la revolución!" But that didn't happen until Uncle Carlos died.

In her younger days, only whores ran around singing at palenques with Lucha Villa, and Abuela Chucha and Abuelo Pancho objected to their daughter running around in the company of married men with tequila on their breath and pockets bulging with pesos. A daughter was disowned if her parents didn't approve of her parrandera lifestyle. And that's what happened to Tía Alicia. Once married to her sweetheart, when Alicia arrived at her parents' home with a busted lip, Abuela Chucha responded, "That's your cross." With broken dreams,

Tía Alicia left for El Norte with her husband, who gave her two permanent black stars for eyes and a welted purple body.

For years, without parents and a face, Uncle Carlos, a tall man with long arms and large hands, broke Tía Alicia while she fended for herself with a broom, a mop, an iron, and six children. With a swollen belly, she blocked the kicks from striking her stomach. Slowly like a parrot that loses its instinct to sing from too much abuse, Alicia in the company of her man lost her parents, her brothers, her sisters, and her voice.

If her husband snapped his fingers, that meant "Right now—in this instant, Pendeja—if you don't want me to beat the shit out of you when we get home." She blamed the bruises on her arm on a supposed Tonka truck Betito had thrown at her. Other times she blamed the yellowish green blotches underneath the gauze to too much cleaning. Tía Alicia survived thirty years of spit words ricocheting her body—of being kicked and yanked by her hair. There were other women like Tía Alicia who didn't sing their grief and didn't have the same luck as their husbands dying.

"Y adios adios
adios adios
que tengas suerte en la vida"

El Diablo

Juan Páramo "El Diablo" had already graduated from high school but cruised after school to check out the teenage girls. Diablo constantly threatened and loomed over my father because boys—men—could alter our destiny. That's why Paloma, Crucito, "Our Chaperone," and I left St. Mark's Annual Fair that summer day when word had it Diablo was on his way to church "looking for Sofia." By the time we reached home, Juan had already written his name on Dad's dusty Monte Carlo parked in front of our house: "'Diablo was here. c/s.'"

The holy water on his forehead had already dried up. Diablo wasn't red or carried a pitchfork like the one in the Lotería and metal retablo paintings. Unlike other teenage boys, Diablo looked only into my eyes and nowhere else, and that scared me. His mischievous smile framed his cholo mustache and goatee. El Diablo's mind went to imaginary places I didn't understand, not even from watching love scenes in American movies, Mexican soap operas, or reading books all combined.

What I needed to remember were Father's consejos—his words I could never forget. *It's not that he loves you; it's that he wants to fuck you.*

To a boy, as Dad had warned, a girl became a soccer ball, "como una pelota de fútbol," he wished to kick around and

score a few goals with, so his buddies would cheer him on—
and add more points to the team's scoreboard.

Juan persisted and wouldn't give up. One day on a week-
night, Diablo knocked on our front door—I was already
sleeping. That's how late it was. Juan Páramo with his Pedro
Armendáriz arching eyebrows and bullet eyes came face to face
with my father, whose reputation had made him notorious
for his overprotectiveness and recalcitrant tone. Paloma said
Father's eyes bulged out as he stared at the "good-for-nothing
pendejo" standing in our doorway.

"Good evening, Señor. You must be Sofia's father. Is Sofia
home?"

"Who-are-you? And-WHAT-do-YOU-need-Sofia-for?"

"I'm Sofia's classmate. We go to school together. I need to
ask your daughter a question about our biology homework?"

"Your homework? Muchachito, do-you-know-what-time-it-is?"

"No, Señor. Umm—I think it's seven o'clock."

"SEVEN? IT'S 9:30 IN THE EVENING, PENDEJO!"

On San Marcos Boulevard, by the time Diablo hopped into
his white Monte Carlo lowrider with a replica of the Virgen de
Guadalupe on his hood and revved his engine, Juan blasted his
stereo with "I do love you, I love you, I love you, yes, I do girl,"
Paloma woke me up to tell me about El Diablo's visit.

After their brief exchange, Juan "como alma que lo llevaba el
diablo" ran to his lowrider, parked behind our family's Monte
Carlo. In front of our house, Diablo hopped and danced his
Monte Carlo to taunt my father and show off his hydraulics.
In my bedroom facing the boulevard, I ran in circles and then
to the bathroom because I was suffering from "córrele que te

alcanza"—the runs—and Dad was fuming. *How was I supposed to explain to my father I really didn't know Diablo? Would Dad even believe me if I told him the truth?*

Days and months went by, and Dad never confronted me about Juan "El Diablo" Páramo.

Peacocks and Snakes Too

Men. Dad didn't like chavalos like Diablo or men like our neighbor, Don Cipriano Manríquez. He lived over on El Desierto Street. He controlled his wife so much she acted like a child—needy. Mrs. Manríquez needed her husband to do everything for her: take her to the grocery store because she didn't know how to drive. Don Cipriano took his wife to the mall to buy her dresses because she didn't earn money or own a car of her own. And whenever Don Cipriano dressed his wife, he always acted so flamboyant, spreading his wings like a peacock. Don Cipriano Manríquez acted like "puro pájaro nalgón." Peacocks could fly—but not long distances.

Wives had to ask their husbands for permission to do *everything*. Todito.

"Can you buy some more diapers for the baby?"

"Can you buy Toñito a new pair of shoes?"

"Can you buy me a new dress for Mother's Day?"

"Can you buy me a new blender?"

Men like Don Cipriano didn't know *they* were the needy ones—like children—not adults. They needed a wife to cook for them. They needed a wife to iron their clothes. They needed a wife to bring them a towel, underwear, socks, and toilet paper.

Men like Don Cipriano acted like peacocks and snakes too. They shed their skin everywhere—in the bathroom, in the living room, in their bedroom, and including in the kitchen. A boot here, a stinky sock over there, a dirty plate here—the shedding was endless and would never stop unless the vecinas stopped picking after their husbands and sons. But oh, what would his family and the neighbors say if Don Cipriano's wife, la Señora Manríquez, stopped cleaning and cooking for her husband?

"She's a dirty woman."

"She doesn't clean her house."

"Look at how that poor man lives. That nasty woman doesn't clean for him. She doesn't deserve him. Vive en un palacio y no limpia su casa. Es una cochina."

Don Cipriano needed a wife to ask him to open a jar of preserved nopales. How else would his wife cook for him? *She could not survive without him. Driving was so difficult and so dangerous—she was bound to get into a car accident.* That's what Don Cipriano wanted his wife to believe. And Mrs. Manríquez started believing it.

One day I noticed it wasn't just Don Cipriano—Don Pedro and Mr. Jones were playing their part too. It was beyond my neighborhood and little, tall, and big women of all shapes and colors played their part in little and big houses too.

On TV, after dinner, while watching a detergent commercial, I saw a little girl tell her mother, "Mom, one day I want to wash clothes like you!" Dad muttered with alcohol on his breath, "Stupid girl. She doesn't know what she's saying."

Parrot in the Oven

Both Paco and Dad had clairvoyant powers. Paco, our parrot, predicted when Dad would arrive home from work with beer in his belly and an argument. Dad predicted Domingo Sietes. Seventh Sundays. When Dad would turn the street corner on San Marcos Boulevard, Paco always sang excitedly and danced in his cage. Lately, when Dad raised his voice, even in the company of guests, from his black iron cage, Paco's little head bobbed back and forth in defiance. His orange-red eyes pinned as he fluffed and flared his bright green wings; then, Paco, alone and standing competed with Dad's ethanol screams as our perico sidestepped and weaved side to side. Dad complained about our green-headed parrot, but at least Paco didn't get drunk and talk about unplanned pregnancies at family gatherings.

"Compadre, if my daughters, Paloma and Sofia, come home with a Domingo Siete, I'm kicking them out of the house," Dad swore, holding a beer up in the air at our family's communal space, our kitchen table.

"No, Compadrito. You can't do that. You can't say that because it hasn't happened to your daughters. That's why you say that, Compadrito, because it hasn't happened to you."

"That's how it's going to be, Compadre. Paloma! Shut that pinche perico up or take him outside, or else I'm going to make him fly!" Dad screamed as he punched and kicked the air. "Don't tell me no, Compadre. I don't care. They'll have to leave! Like my mother used to say, 'Si quieren azul celeste, que les cueste. ¡Que se vayan mucho a la chingada!'" Dad warned. And we knew he would stick to his word if we ever dishonored our Mexican Catholic family's reputation.

Praying did not ward off the Seventh Sunday. It angered Paloma and me when Father talked about us publicly and cast spells on girls we knew, especially *the smart ones*, who attended Sunday mass and church retreats. "You'll see—pretty soon she'll get pregnant," Dad would assure us. And, shockingly, he was always right. Even the good girls, the ones whose parents afforded expensive quinceañeras and were devout church goers, didn't escape a Domingo Siete. As soon as teenage girls, some of them our friends and acquaintances, couldn't hide the bloating, they disappeared and dropped out of school—sometimes as early as middle school. Other times, their parents took them far away on a vacation. Some of these girls returned with flat bellies, a sign a girl's parents took care of what had happened on a Seventh Sunday.

As far as Paco's clairvoyant powers, we figured it out. Paco heard the whistling sound coming from Dad's Monte Carlo a mile away. For Paco listening to Father's car sounded like hearing a tea kettle announcing scalding bubbles, and Paloma and I ran to the safety of our room.

For us, Paco's loud squawking signaled to go hide in our bedroom, sleep like butterflies, and stay vigilant, always, for a lurking predator. In case Dad cracked the door open and demanded a meeting that extended for hours at the dinner table. In our room, facing the wall, we acted as if we were asleep. On our beds, with our eyes wide open, we tilted our heads downward. Paloma and I didn't know yet, but our wings weren't clipped like Paco's, and we were both ready—just in case anything happened.

The S and the M Fly

The woman looked at me as I placed $17.50 on the counter for a pair of black cowboy boots, a novel, and a copper winged locket I found at the thrift store next to the Vons on East San Marcos Boulevard across San Marcos High School. On the cover of *The Awakening*, a woman stood alone facing a desolate beach. At the counter, with her reading glasses slipping off her nose and her hands knitting an iridescent ball of yarn with two needles, she stared at me and glanced at the items on the counter with her beady gray eyes. She asked, "Would you like me to read your name?"

"*My name?*"

"Yes, I can read your signature—your penmanship."

"Sure." *Why not?* I thought.

She slipped a small yellow piece of lined paper across the counter, and I nervously wrote my name as sloppy as I could, so I could confuse her. *About what?* I didn't know.

"Sofia Martinez. Do you know what your name means?"

"Umm—no."

"Your name means wisdom. You're an artist. Do you draw?"

"No—not really."

"Your writing is legible. You've come to this world to communicate. Don't be afraid. Look at the way your S and M fly and curl outward. That means you're a creative person. *Do you write?*"

"Write? Nope. Not really. Just schoolwork—I wrote about my uncle making fun of my hair for my English class. *Does that count?*"

"Only you will know. Look at the way your writing slants to the right—that's a sign you always move forward with everything you do. But look at the way your last name, Martinez, goes back and overlaps with your name, Sofia."

"Is that *bad?*"

"No. Not necessarily. That means the past is always present in your future. Look at the way you dot your 'i' and cross your 't.' That's a sign you're determined, and you're in control of your life. *What do you think?*"

"A lot of people tell me my signature is pretty, and they ask me if I went to Catholic School, but I'm not really sure why I write the way I do."

"It's in you. You'll see. Come back."

It's in me? What did the woman mean when she said, "'It's in you'"?

The woman handed me a white plastic bag with my purchase and a small receipt. As I walked out through the thrift store's glass doors, I could feel the ocean breeze on my cheeks.

I wasn't sure why the woman picked me or if she asked all the thrift store's customers the same question. As I walked home, I remembered the time my kindergarten teacher dragged my little brown body by the arm across the room as I cried and gasped for air in a corner of the classroom for two reasons: I couldn't write my name and couldn't speak English. As much as I tried writing the first letter of my name, the "S" looked like a backward reflection in a mirror, and my first-grade teacher sent me to the white trailer to perfect my English.

As I walked home, ignoring the honking and whistling coming from passing cars on San Marcos Boulevard, I thought about my penmanship—I thought about my parents and how they identified landmarks for directions when we traveled. My parents had learned to memorize the spelling of their names even though they couldn't read or write. And when the school would send forms that needed a signature, we always preferred Mom's signature over Dad's because his writing looked like a miniature version of the Himalayas.

Mother's signature, on the other hand, was complete. Although her signature took her at least two minutes to write, Mom signed her name beautifully. Her cursive writing, her curved capital letters, the H in Helena and the M in Martinez, were elegant like her sewing. *That's* where my signature came from, I thought. *But what did the part about the past in the present mean?*

"Go back to Mexico!"

Although the afternoon was cold with a few dark clouds blotching the sky, the sun illuminated the sidewalk and the shiny black car jetting by. We were picketing silently at first when one of those things that if I told somebody, especially my mother, no one would ever believe me. It was like if I told someone I had seen a UFO, like saying I had won the lottery, or swearing I had seen Bigfoot on a camping trip.

Irma, my church friend and coworker, and I had been marching in unison on the sidewalk parallel to Discovery Street next to St. Mark's Church and the fancy mobile park because the Spanish speaking community wanted Father Diego, who was bilingual, to stay his full term. But instead St. Mark's would be replacing him with a priest who only spoke English. With handheld signs, Irma, a small group of people, and I implored: "LET FATHER DIEGO STAY! LET FATHER DIEGO STAY! LET FATHER DIEGO STAY! OUR COMMUNITY DESERVES A SPANISH SPEAKING PRIEST!" And I don't know what made the priest with white hair, gold rimmed glasses, and sunken cheeks think no one would ever find out what he hollered from his black Mercedes Benz's passenger car window: "Go back to Mexico!"

Had that really been a priest peering his head and screaming from the Mercedes's window? That man couldn't have been a priest.

I never thought a holy man, *a man of God*, could ever say such words: "Go back to Mexico!"

What did the signs we were holding have to do with México?

Our mouths dropped as Irma and I stared at each other in disbelief. But our eyes hadn't played tricks on us and neither had our ears. We had both seen his face and heard his callous words. One of us could have been a victim, but the two of us were witnesses.

Hours later overcast clouds set in. From my memory, I erased a man, wearing a black clerical shirt and a white roman collar, like a photographer spots a speck of dust on a black and white photograph. I looked away in search of a larger universe. Nothing hid from the full moon's silvery beams or the sun's rays—not even a priest on a cloudy day.

When I got home, I went straight to my mom's Vaporú smelling room. In her bedroom, when I told her about the church incident on Discovery Street, she faced her wooden cross, blessed herself three times, and prayed a "Padre Nuestro" for herself and me. Ironically, my parents had taught me the Ten Commandments, and I took the eighth to heart. In Spanish, "No dirás falsos testimonios ni mentirás," and in English, "Thou shalt not bear false witness against thy neighbor." In either Spanish or English, a lie was a lie.

Before I walked out of my mother's room, I gave her a heads up, "Oh, Amá, by the way, a journalist approached Irma and me and asked if he could add our photograph to the *San Diego Times*—the picture he took at the protest—to his article. We said, 'Yes.'" Mother blessed herself and pleaded, "Ay Sofia, go talk to la Virgencita."

What was I supposed to talk to la Virgencita about—that Irma and I had done the right thing for protesting and telling the journalist our truth and nothing but the truth?

NOW HIRING

I said goodbye to Joey's Tacos and got hired because my friend, Irma, put in a good word for me to the owner at Sandwich Alley on East San Marcos Boulevard. Irma didn't want me to work at the fake-taco-place anymore after she heard about the pest problem.

On my second day on the job, I quickly learned lazy teenagers, who got hired, usually got fired or quit by the first week of work. Hector, a co-worker, at twenty-three had at least seven years of fast-food experience. He didn't work in the fields like his father who picked strawberries in Carlsbad's strawberry fields, but Hector sure did work hard, just like his Mexican father and my father. Instead of picking strawberries and potatoes with an arched back, we added lettuce, pickles and tomatoes to sandwiches. Hector worked full-time at Sandwich Alley and attended the local community college across the train tracks by the large P for Palomar, a landmark on a hill on the northside of San Marcos that meant dovecote in Spanish.

Every now and then, the owner posted a yellow NOW HIRING sign facing the boulevard. The same teenager always stopped by to ask, "Are you hiring?" while I took the sandwich bread out of the oven, and Hector restocked the prep table with lettuce and tomatoes. We both locked eyes and heard the owner say, "Sorry. I'm getting ready to pull the NOW HIRING sign down." Immediately, Hector and I stared at each other in disbelief because we both knew the owner had just fired one of the newbies.

We were hiring. Why didn't the owner want to hire the Black teenager? She hired White people and Latinos. Why not the African American teenager?

While I worked at Sandwich Alley, the owner never hired the Black teenager, who probably attended the local high school and who I imagined had dreams of attending college like Hector, Irma, and me. Our boss hired teenage White surfers and hippies who attended college. Irma, lighter than the Black teenager and I got hired. When incidents like that happened at Sandwich Alley, I wanted to call a phone number to report our boss, but I had no idea where to call or what to do about the big yellow sign in front of Sandwich Alley facing the boulevard.

At Joey's Tacos, cockroaches had been a problem, and now at Sandwich Alley the NOW HIRING sign that didn't hire certain people was a problem both Hector's eyes and my eyes could see.

The Leftovers

At break, wearing bold and bright colors, big shirts, and baggy jeans, Black teens of all shades hung out in front of the library, where they chilled and busted moves to the electrifying beats of hip hop from a boombox. During break and lunch, cholos hung out next to the bathroom, where they guarded the fortress with one knee bent up and their backs leaning against the wall. Under their black shades, cholos, dressed in khaki pants and white T-shirts or tank tops. Cholos checked out the girls as they walked in and out of the bathroom. Then, there were the football players, stamped with their magic blue jerseys and Ray-Ban sunglasses. They were the school's timeless Disney hall passes parading San Marcos High School with smiles, hand waves, and high fives.

Next to the football field in our portable classrooms, English teachers were dry, proper—correct like standard American English. Every day in our English class, we opened our bible-thick books. Symbols, metaphors, and hidden meanings were in everything we read. Fitzgerald's writing was green, and Curley filled his glove with Vaseline to keep his hand soft. *For what?* I kept trying to figure out. Custodians were the friendlier folk on campus. Their faces matched my skin and spared a few words unlike SMHS office staff who ignored us unless we asked for a pass.

As an office aide, I walked in and out of classrooms, and for the first time, I witnessed a VIP lecture. For a second, I thought I had walked into the wrong class. Making jokes and wearing a navy-blue letterman jacket, Mr. Colton, the rookie and former football star player with a crew cut, was on a teaching high. I couldn't help but notice he was not the same teacher who taught the morning class, where I sat and took notes for students during second period. Entranced, Mr. Colton's blue eyes enjoyed the limelight as his one-man show brightened the classroom.

That day—I noticed students in his afternoon class matched his skin color, and I understood the high school caste system. Mr. Colton's melodramatic soliloquy—his two-thumbs up performance—entertained "the cool kids" at San Marcos High School. For Mr. Colton, the morning class I sat in to take notes was a struggle to teach and a mental strain. The teenagers who made up the morning class were the school's leftovers.

Nobody wanted to teach the leftovers; those students made teachers' careers challenging and boring. I wondered if the thrown paper wads and gum on the ceiling in my classes meant I had been a leftover my freshman, sophomore, and junior year in high school. Leftovers always tasted better, but at San Marcos High School, they produced a sour and bitter taste to teachers' mouths.

The Wind in My Hair

At the beach, the colors are soft—creamy hues of blues, browns, and pinks. The wind wraps itself and then releases the black strands of my long dark wavy hair as if it plays a harp between its fingers. This song is about me—the one who resides inside me, Sofia, the one who wears a seashell collar necklace.

Hector and I run side by side hand in hand. The foamy water kisses our feet. I smile. I let go of his grip and laugh without saying a word. There are no words but echoing laughs. The tickling sensation caressing my toes makes me laugh again. I smile at Hector. Hector returns my smile and continues running, not ahead of me—beside me.

Our legs are not tired. They don't feel the sand under our feet or anything around us. From a distance, the wind pulls at our bodies like a tornado slowly and softly tugging at trees. We don't care if the water is cold because we are together—running freely along the shore on this limitless beach.

I am naked. Hector is naked. And we are running.

I am not embarrassed or ashamed—exposed—for the world to see.

I open my eyes to my mother hovering over me and to the sunlight's piercing rays peeking through the curtains, blinding me.

"Buenosss díasss Chofi. *Wake up*. It's eleven o'clock in the morning. Ya está el desayuno."

"Sorry Amá. After I got home from work, I stayed up late watching Arsenio Hall and Johnny Canales on TV."

"Cuéntame. ¿Qué soñaste?"

"Nada Ma—I don't remember what I dreamed about."

"Chofi, levántate flojita. Ya vente a comer. Y después te pones a buscar unos tomatillos para hacer una salsa verde para la cena."

"Sí Ma—ya voy. Deme unos minutitos."

I pull the covers over me and turn my body over. With my hands, I take the pillow and press it against the back of my head and suffocate my fluttering hair. I don't tell my mother, our official dream reader, or Hector about this dream. This one I will call "The Wind in My Hair." This one I will keep to myself.

I close my eyes, press REWIND, PLAY, and then REPEAT.

That Sunday morning, I learned the hidden language of dreams—the ones that hid from Mom and Dad, especially Dad, in plain sight.

Teachers and Cops

White teachers scared me, especially White male teachers.

"You know the answers," Mr. Boehner with opaque blue eyes assured me as I stared nervously at the test with a circus of numbers and symbols somersaulting in different directions. (I hadn't told Mr. Boehner I couldn't see the chalkboard from my desk because he would reassign me another seat, and I would have to change places and sit closer to him while he lectured.) Mr. Boehner—a thin, pale teacher—stood beside me feeding me the answers as I retook the test. When I was done, I left the beige-colored classroom feeling uneasy.

As I walked to the front of the school, I noticed Mr. Boehner kept staring at me from his car as he held his hands on the steering wheel, so I took refuge at a nearby payphone near the main office on school grounds. Through the fingerprints and graffiti placas, I stared at my smudgy reflection and pretended I was dialing and calling Dad to pick me up.

"Buenooooo. ¿Quién habla?"

"Hola, Apá. Ya salí. ¿Me puede recojer de la escuela, por favor?"

Months later, in my Economics class, on my first day of summer school, Mr. Fields decided I wouldn't have to take tests. Because, according to Mr. Fields, I was "too smart for tests," he promoted me to class treasurer.

During one of those hot summer school days, Mr. Fields gave me a ripe soft purple plum. It felt awkward to hold the juicy tender flesh in my hand, so I didn't eat it. Ripe avocados had been a problem when I was twelve, and now at seventeen a squishy, ripe plum felt awkward in my sweaty hand. For the entire summer, I collected a quarter a day from each student for our Economics class project. And with that money, I bought a 6-foot Sandwich from work at the end of summer for the entire class.

Then, at Sandwich Alley, a regular, a White cop with gold rimmed glasses, made my stomach churn. He had never struck a conversation until the day I swept the lobby while he ate his sandwich. The cop asked me as he stared at me, "Do you know *why* I eat here?" I shrugged my shoulders. In a dry tone, he answered, "So I can watch you sweep," as his wolf eyes fixed on me, and he slowly chewed the pastrami sandwich I had prepared with my own hands.

When the cop said those words, I kept sweeping and mopping fast like a windshield wiper on a gloomy, rainy day, so I could move out of his peripheral vision and barricade myself behind the counter.

I could forget the name on his name tag and shiny badge but could never forget his face in a lineup.

Emiliano Martinez or Any Other Name

To some people, Spanish names made no sense.

In high school, four sisters were all named María. The Marías included María de los Ángeles (Mary of Angels like the city of Los Ángeles), María Candelaria (Mary of Candles), María Guadalupe (The Mexican Virgin Mary Coatlalopeuh), and María Concepción (Mary Conception) to name a few Catholic names. They weren't the only ones.

Other Marías didn't have a choice. My mother's full name was Maria Helena Ramirez de Avila, but she preferred Helena Martinez to keep it short and simplify paperwork in the United States (because she had to learn to write her name). At school, a classmate's father had wanted to name her Navidad because she had been born on December 25th. But Mexican registrar officials insisted Navidad was not a Christian name and forced her parents to name her, María Navidad, (literally in English— Mary Christmas). And so it was.

Or how about the first-time father who unfolded a small piece of paper and handed it to a nurse in México. His daughter's name proudly written in bold letters not to forget the spelling, **H a i r y**. And because his newborn had been named in a Spanish-speaking country, no one stopped him from naming his daughter, Hairy. In Spanish, Hairy did sound like Heidi. *Didn't it?*

Hairy . . . Heidi.

American names, like "Hairy" instead of Heidi, were Span-ish-speaking parents' obsession. Some parents named their children American names they pronounced like fish flopping in their mouths.

"No way Jose!" got slapped after José. Hoe-say meant "Nothing for you Ho-say!" *Nada.* Zippo. Nothing. Forget about it! No way Hoe-say—not an inch.

I remember seeing a new classmate confused when he intro-duced himself: "Hello, I'm Jesús. You can call me Chuy. Nice to meet you." And a smart ass in our English class responded, "Yeah and I'm Luke Skywalker." Jesús had said, "Chuy," *not Chewbacca!*

And teachers didn't understand why sound parents named their child Adolfo "like Adolf Hitler" or Benito "like Benito Mussolini." Adolfo—not *Adolf.* And *Benito*—after Benito Juárez, the first Indigenous president of México. Names didn't make sense to English speakers who didn't want to take the time to learn to pronounce names correctly.

One day I would name my children cool sounding superhe-ro names like Cuauhtémoc, Fonz, Alondra, Eréndira or Cleo-patra. Anything but a common name, so my children wouldn't believe it. Because if names really didn't mean anything, why hadn't my parents named me after Emiliano Zapata? Emiliano or Emiliana Martinez. Names. Not Reymundo like my Uncle Mundo, or else I'd think I was the King of the World—invinci-ble—and get in lots of trouble. *Not Juan*, perhaps, Juancho, so kids at school wouldn't tell me: Juan, two, three.

Tomasito

"En la sala de un hospital
a las 9:43 nació Simón.
Es el verano del 56
el gran orgullo de don Andrés
por ser varón".
—Willie Colón, "Simón, el gran varón"

Tomasito. I saw him running across the lawn at school today. He wore black eyeliner like his sisters and girl cousins. His eyelids were puffy like he had just woken up, and his eyelashes were long and curled upward. With half-closed eyes, Tomasito's eyes gazed like actresses in Mexican soap operas.

In the morning right before the tardy bell rang, he sprinted eloquently like a deer in pink sneakers as a hundred pair of eyes shot him down. Tomasito. *He carried a red purse and wore short shorts just like girls. Who did Tomasito like? How had Tomasito learned to walk like that? Where had Tomasito learned to run like that? Did boys and girls tell him hurt words?*

Dad told me a story about someone like Tomasito—Víctor. Víctor was Dad's childhood friend. Years later, when Father visited his hometown, he heard the news. Víctor had been macheted to death.

No one saved him.

And I never forgot what everyday people could do to people like Simón en el extranjero, Víctor in Michoacán, and Tomasito in Alta California.

Tomasito, did you get married?
Where are you?
Do you have children?
Did you change your name?
Are you okay?
Are you alive?

Big Bad Wolves

I remember no one wanted to talk about it at our school. Nobody could believe this happened in our town, but it did. These boys let themselves in on you. No one told them it wasn't right to shove a remote control between your legs. Lindsey Getman, pobre huerita with crystal blue eyes and soft blonde hair. No one heard you whimper in that room, where teenage boys turned into big bad wolves circling in on you, clawing at you with their dirty fingernails, and spitting you with words.

Did they put something in your drink? Why did these boys put a broom where babies are born? Did they think their grandmothers, mothers, sisters, and girlfriends would never find out? When you woke up, did you remember their ugly faces and ugly laughs? Did you need a bucket of ice to sit on for the bleeding and pain to stop? When you went home, did your Momma and Poppa hold you in their arms as your tears wet their red faces, or did they push you away? And, Lindsey, when you looked at yourself in the mirror, did you want to clean your smudgy reflection with hollow eyes, staring back and want to run and hide in a forest under a cypress tree? Did *anyone* at your new high school find out?

Cholas Falsas

As Paloma and I walked home from school and approached our house, we noticed Dad's car in the driveway.

That was strange. Dad never took days off even if he had a hangover. What was Dad doing home so early?

Standing in the doorway with his arms crossed and chest puffed out, Dad screamed, "Paloma and Sofia Martinez, sit down at the table right now! We need to talk," as his wagging index finger directed us to the kitchen table.

Even though we didn't know what Dad wanted to bring our attention to, Paloma started chewing her fingernails. I could feel my ears warming up and my top lip quivering. We both knew we hadn't done anything wrong at school. We knew better. But judging from Dad's angry demeanor, it didn't look good. Whatever he was going to scold us about was bad—really bad—because Dad turned into a giant lobster with huge red claws ready to eat us alive.

"¡Mister Goldberg me llamó de la escuela y tuve que ir a su oficina!" *Dad had to take the day off because of us?*

"Our principal, Mr. Goldberg, called you in the office today? *WHY?*"

"¡SÍ! ¡Ya les dije que no me hablen inglés!"

"¡El director dice que tú, Paloma, y tu hermana son cholas!"

"*¿Cholas?*" asked Paloma.

A nervous chuckle escaped my mouth because Mr. Golberg had pulled a funny one, but it wasn't funny because Dad was furious.

"No te rías, Sofia Martinez. ¡SÍ! ¡Dijo que las dos son cholas!"

"But Dad—that's not true!"

"How are you *not* cholas? What do you want people to believe when they see your peacock hair and baggy pants?"

"Dad—but all the girls our age wear their hair and clothes like us."

"Yeah Dad. You drive a Monte Carlo, and our friends say that you drive a cholo car, but you're not a cholo. *Are you?*"

"Shut up Sofia! Stay quiet. I'm not very happy with both of you right now. *This isn't about me or the other girls.* This is about *you* TWO!"

"Dad, did they call other parents too? What did you tell Mr. Goldberg?" Paloma asked.

"I told the principal my daughters grew up in Vista and San Marcos—that I know my own daughters well, and that you two are not cholas—and if he could please give me details on this gang of yours I didn't know about," Dad lowered his voice by the end of his reprimand. "Go to your room ahorita! Your Mom is getting home, and I don't want her to worry about this. We'll talk about this later tonight after dinner."

In our room, Paloma and I started laughing at our principal—because he thought we were "C H O L AS." He was no princi-*pal* of ours. How could Mr. Goldberg think he knew more about us than we did? *Who did he think he was? God?*

Some girls changed into a different pair of clothes at school. We didn't have to do that. At home, we teased our hair with a hair pick, sprayed our bangs with Aqua Net, and fanned out our hair. The higher our bangs—the better. And yes, we wore black baggy pants, but that was our style—even Janet Jackson wore baggy pants. Paloma and I wore black liquid eyeliner and outlined our lips with black eyeliner pencil and added burgundy or red lipstick and even Mom wore burgundy lipstick on special occasions. When we went out shopping for back-to-school clothes, Mom and Dad allowed us to pick our own clothing, but they always made sure the clothes we picked weren't oversized, especially Cruz's clothes.

Cholas hung out after school. We didn't have permission to do anything after school, except to come straight home to clean, to help Cruz with his homework, to do our homework, to water the trees in the backyard, to start cooking dinner, and to work part time after school. We weren't tatted up or part of an *official gang*—the type that has to jump you in like Varrio San Marcos or Varrio South Los Angeles as Mr. Goldberg claimed.

We didn't live la vida loca. We lived *la vida boring!* No prom. No homecoming. No sleepovers. No get-togethers. No nada de nada.

Our Martinez cousins were the real cholos and cholas—not us. At school, we could throw down if anyone started any trouble with us, but Mr. Goldberg's eyes couldn't see Paloma and I were from the Cholas Falsas Crew.

Locked Up in the Mind

"Roses are the Mexican's favorite flower. I think, how symbolic—thorns and all."
—Gloria Anzaldúa, *Borderlands/La Frontera: The New Mestiza*

She lost him before she even knew it. Tía Alicia lost her son, Primo Beto, to the letters carved on his stomach, the size of freeway signs, announcing cities and streets from faraway distances. With those drawings under his clothes and skin, he relived the beatings, echoing in his memory like the lighter burning the melting brown rock on a spoon, easing the pain only he felt. Too much trippin' locked Primo Beto up in the mind, like the hamster that overfeeds itself and doesn't know when to stop eating—and dies. But our cousin Beto didn't die. He's locked up in the mind and behind bars.

Back then, if you talked to him, he stared at you but not like he was your cousin or your own son. Beto looked at you to see how you could feed his addiction (with your VCR, TV, toolbox, or blender). That's only part of the reason he's locked up in la grande in solitary confinement, doing prison time. Tía Alicia has hope—the kind only a mother understands. The kind only *she* understands because her hope reads backwards when I see him.

"Betito. He was a good boy."

Maybe, Mom's right when she says people bring their children to this country in search of better lives and their dreams. But instead, children are lost and yearn for a real family while their parents take care of someone else's kids. While parents work overtime to pay the bills, their children waste away in the streets as beggars of praise and acceptance.

In hardworking parents' minds, their children don't work when they study: they're not working—not with arched backs, not with a shovel or a mop in between their hands. Parents are so tired they don't want to talk about school. Instead, they stare at the lives of pretty, rich people on TV and wake up at dawn to beat the traffic, so they can keep their bosses happy. Because if they miss a day or are late to work, people like my parents get fired. But *they* can take days off, of course, and rest when they're sick. *Not us.*

"He *was* a good boy," Tía Alicia says. When I hear her talk like that, I can see she's locked up in the mind too, but she has a mother's faith.

Tía Alicia doesn't understand how her son's mind works. In front of her doorsteps, he sees signs and colors. The Lutheran Church divides the west and the east side: The Vatos Locos del Westside and The Vatos Locos del Eastside patrolled their ground. She doesn't see that. She can't. Primo Beto claimed a hood that belongs to no one—like the air we breathe. (*Don't breathe. It's my air. How does that sound?*) Just like governments mark green, white, yellow, red, and blue lines to divide streets and borders with man-made fences.

Tía Alicia says Beto had a good girlfriend who dressed him well, but she gave up on him when Beto said he wouldn't be going to college. The last time I saw him he looked sharp—bien catrín—in his creased pants, black shiny shoes de charol, and Three Flower slicked black hair like he worked at a bank.

The Primo Betos of today are easy, necessary targets to play the game of pistolitas and mad doggers. Like an angry grizzly bear, his stare really kills. Don't stare too long, or there will be claws. His generation and the next generation fill up prison cells instead of classrooms. They sit lined up against the curb, looking like real bad asses with a police officer calling up for backup and hoping to find background on the bait.

For what?

Primo Beto might as well have had a real bullet tattooed to the side of his temple or his neck; that's what his uniform did.

I heard Primo Beto isn't just locked up in the mind but behind bars in another country. He got that tattoo on his face after the incident—trying to stop his father from fucking his daughter. Beto finally had the courage to strike his own father. With an iron, Beto struck him on the temple.

If a stranger looked at my cousin, he'd be scared. I'm not. Every tattoo tells Beto's story like the crosses, the thorns, paintings, and statues at churches. Like a church, he decorates his body with memories of pain. His body is a war and peace zone of both visual and written languages, a miscommunication of sorts. Because numbers, words, and images spoken and written on his own brown body, according to him, are worth sacrificing for, like most faithful soldiers. Without a doubt in their mind, they are fighting a just war.

Behind bars, Primo Beto circles and circles like a caged bear at the zoo. He will never feel a chilly night tug at his skin. He waits in vain for the cage to open to recreate his life now that his father is dead. But now, he's locked up in the mind and behind himself.

"He was a good boy . . . he gave me a rose for Mother's Day when he was five."

Green Dollar Dreams

"Soñaba que yo era rico
que en mis bolsillos llevaba
muchos billetes de a mil
y que un mariachi tocaba
las canciones más bonitas
que te gustaban a ti."
—Rosendo Gutiérrez Martínez, "Billetes de a mil"

There were other types of men who were lost like Primo Beto but instead were searching for green dollar dreams.

Tired from spending the weekend in Rosarito, Uncle David flew north on I-15 with a full tank of gas. This time he made no pit stops. Going 85 mph, he listened to the usual, the crooning of The King of Mexican country, Vicente Fernández. Ever since the day Padre Homero had blessed Uncle David's family RV in front of St. Rose Church for a $20.00 donation, La Consentida had never failed him.

The man, searching for a pot of green dollars on the U.S. side, held onto the rooftop of La Consentida, Uncle David's RV, as if his life depended on it—*and it did*. On the RV's rooftop, the man's muscles became taut from the burning sensation, making it impossible to fidget because he told his fingers to remain clasped, at all costs. If they disobeyed and listened to the cramps, at any sudden stop, his body would shoot like a human rocket and plaster itself on an American freeway. His face stooped low to avoid the wind from whipping his face and drying out his eyes. The memory of his wife and children's smiles fleeted at the thought of his body hitting the black asphalt—his family would never find out if . . . he died.

When La Consentida arrived in Vista, as usual, the family unpacked the camping gear and looked forward to a hot shower, a cup of Chocolate Ibarra and sweet Mexican bread. And then, as if he were drunk, the man stumbled down the RV's ladder. The family could see his body and feet were limp from the metal rungs pressing against his body.

Bewildered, Uncle David stood at an incredible sight and the thought of a migra back in Tijuas catching a paisano on his registered owned vehicle. Who would believe his story—of a man holding onto his Consentida—for an opportunity to join the masses, working for green dollar dreams?

The man with a sun-beaten face with hollow-dark eyes bemoaned, "*Señor.*" Not giving the man enough time to speak, Uncle David interrupted the man as he reached for his pockets and found foreign coins, a few dollars, and spare change. Avoiding eye contact with the stranger, my uncle dropped American change in his hand. With a deep-cutting tone, Uncle David interjected, "*Tenga. Por favor, váyase.*" The man silenced his pleas and disappeared between rows of single-story houses on East Indian Rock Street.

La Tanda

In our neighborhood, everyone hustled to make ends meet. It was like drug dealing. Everybody dropped off one hundred dollars by Friday and left quickly. One after another cars pulled up to the sidewalk by our teeter-totter mailbox and dropped off the money at the door. When someone contributed a Tío Benjamín, that meant they were doing pretty good, economically speaking. If people came with a bundle of green Tío Washingtóns, that meant they were struggling to fork out one hundred bucks. You also had the high rollers who requested two tandas. And people like my father who went last hated owing money, and that was the purpose of La Tanda.

Dad paid everything with cash—always cash. That's why our extended family organized tandas, so we wouldn't fall into debt. "I'd rather have a good night's sleep and not suffer from insomnia from having to think how the hell I'm going to make an expensive car payment," Dad insisted. "Here, in Gringolandia, you buy something on credit and when you finally own it—it breaks or falls apart on you."

That's why my parents paid cash for Mom's car, our Monte Carlo that wasn't so brand new anymore. But Dad didn't care if our car was falling apart—it didn't matter because he didn't owe anybody money. Nada. Nadita. Zippo. That's why they came up with La Tanda—it was like credit, but there wasn't any interest or credit debt involved. Tandas were made up of family like compadres, comadres, sisters, and brothers because those were the very people you trusted, and if they screwed you over, you knew where to find them. When I asked Dad, "Is that illegal?" He replied, "Illegal? That's being smart. Not illegal. Even César and Helen Chávez and Dolores Huerta organized credit unions for farm workers."

For the lineup, some organizers raffled numbers. One of Dad's Compadre's father had just passed away, so everyone agreed he deserved the first tanda to help pay off funeral costs. In a few months, Mom and Dad would receive their $1,000 tanda, and that's how we're finally going to take a family trip to México to visit my abuelito, whom I've never met and have only seen in our family albums.

In the Place of Dreams

His eyes were blue. He looked like Santa Claus except this Santa was small framed and could fit down a chimney. During a class lecture, Professor Gawomone with a distinct young man's voice not matching his age asked, "*Where does the comma go? Before or after the but?*" I'm not sure why I glanced away. I knew better. If students looked away, teachers, including professors, usually called on them.

"Sofía?"

"*Before?*"

"That's correct."

I wasn't sure if I knew the answer or if I had guessed correctly. That was one of the differences between high school and college. In college, there were no goofing off games; you were expected to do your homework, follow along, and most importantly—participate. Professors even gave students participation points. Some classrooms looked the same; desks were lined up in single-file rows, and occasionally a nosy spider hung from the ceiling, or a fly flew in the classroom to eavesdrop. Unlike high school though, neither photographs nor trophies decorated college classrooms; instead, posters and flyers promoting big name universities plastered the walls.

While Professor Gawomone, a Vietnam veteran, continued his lecture on commas with chalk in hand, his face transformed into an unhappy troll and charged toward two girls chattering away in the corner next to the classroom's large windows. With his two blue bullets for eyes, Professor Gawomone screamed, "You two, leave the class right now!"

In their haste to slip out the doorway, one of my classmates almost dropped her textbooks. When Professor Gawomone's bluest eyes transformed, my body tensed up and added to the silence in the room. There were no referrals to the principal's office—no warnings. Just like that, Professor Gawomone's blue eyes and words sent a clear message: Get out and don't come back if you're going to be disrespectful!

In Room E-27, sat former high school students who had been the popular teens at San Marcos High School, and it felt wrong to witness the school's King and Queen's fading popularity matched their incorrect answers. The place of dreams our father called college had sidewalks like the ones he paved for expensive track homes in Temecula, benches, trees, and birds like the ones in our own backyard, drinking fountains like the ones in public parks, and 2 or 3 brown professors who looked like me. In college, there were even students whose ages matched my parents' age!

Paloma and I were sitting in our father's prophetic dream—*en el colegio*—distinguishing a verb from a noun, adding appositives and accents to our names, and writing complete sentences: "Paloma and Sofía, the Martínez sisters, are attending college like their parents had always dreamed."

But was college really the place of dreams?

College challenged students, but it didn't seem impossible to earn a degree. In my Chicano Studies class, Dr. Luz Garzón, had lectured on historical facts I had never heard of in my U.S. History class in high school like the 1970's National Chicano Moratorium March. Paloma and I were sitting in the place of dreams, and it felt natural.

Why did our extended family and my manager, Roberto, at Joey's Tacos doubt we were going to college?

We were officially attending the place father had been laughed at for believing, "Mis hijas van a ir al colegio."

And we were attending college.

In class, I wasn't afraid—I was terrified of Gawomone's bluest eyes—until the day he read one of my pieces, "The Dream Story," aloud in class: "In Father's dream, we have food, words, and numbers, so one day we won't have to sign a check with a humble X."

Writing was important like Benito Juárez and Frederick Douglass and Sor Juana Inés de la Cruz and Sojourner Truth and many others like us, learning to read and write and changing the course of history. By the end of my first semester of college, I could see my father had taught me how to read boys' body language, and Professor Gawomone taught me to read the language of paper and books. Professor Gawomone's bluest eyes taught me a comma was not a nuisance; a comma was a BB pellet, and a period was a bullet.

There was power in reading and writing.

To my eyes, the color blue was no longer blue as in Nazi I had feared in high school. Blue was everywhere—in the sky's ever-changing blue, the sea's chameleonic waters, and mother's Virgencita de Guadalupe's blue-green mantle. Blue was just another color, and a semicolon was like a plus sign, stronger than a comma. People. People were like grammar rules. And *that* was dangerous because people wrote and followed rules made up of semicolons, periods, and commas. And grammar rules didn't include footnotes like the ones we were learning in college.

Attending college made me realize I loved children but, perhaps, I didn't want to be a kindergarten teacher. Perhaps, instead, I could major in something that had to do with letters—like English or journalism because my classmates didn't see language on paper like I did. That was my superpower, and it wasn't invisible. I could edit my peer's writing, and they couldn't do the same for me. For many students in my classes, a pencil and paper were their kryptonite. I, on the other hand, saw the world and paper with a different pair of eyes as if I could see words—writing—through a microscope or a magnifying glass, as if I had ultraviolet eyes with a special purpose, and professors could tell.

Dreaming with Aurora

"Ay que bonito es volar
A las dos de la mañana
A las dos de la mañana
Ay que bonito es volar
Ay mamá".
　　　—"La Bruja"

It was November—in the time of memories and dreams. She wore her long black hair down over her shoulders and her favorite white gown touched her calves. Her bare feet were dry like the desert dust, craving for a drop of water. Under the cherimoya tree, she sat on a concrete bench for a few minutes while she took in her surroundings that looked like her home and then continued her journey. She saw the rabbit on the moon peer through the tall almond tree heavy with flowers; its leaves glistened and danced feverishly as she passed by. Even though the smell of eucalyptus trees permeated the backyard, she couldn't smell it as much as she tried. Something else called her—a smell more powerful—the smell of bright orange cempazuchitl flowers.

As she got closer to the backside of the house, she recognized the geranium clay pots lining alongside the house. The estafiate and ruda plants were well taken care of—for a second, she thought they were hers. But as she approached a bedroom window, she saw her face reflected. She didn't know if she was la Llorona or a bruja or the two of them in one. Through her eyes, she didn't look terrifying—not to herself. Looking at her face did startle her a bit, but what startled her most were her feet. They weren't touching the ground. Her body moved slowly, heavy with time on her shoulders, to her altar, where she found her picture in a wooden frame, the only picture of her, the one with her hair tight in a long braid. The candle's flame flickered and the red, bright pink, royal blue, green, and yellow ribbon hanging from the window's frame swayed as she moved to a corner in the living room next to la Virgen de Guadalupe. Her favorite dish—mole rojo, frijoles, and arroz—was still warm with her daughter and granddaughters' hands. Next to the mole, her family had placed a glass of water to quench her thirst. She remembered who she was—she was Aurora. And her granddaughters, Paloma and Sofía, had guided her to the place of the living.

After reuniting with family members placed next to her on the family altar, Aurora then visited Helena, sleeping next to her husband. She found her in the same position she slept as a child. Her Helenita had her beloved Fortino's hair—wavy like the ocean's waves. Staring at her daughter's grown woman's face, Aurora leaned over and kissed her daughter on the forehead. Helena woke up, stayed still and asked, "*¿Mamá, eres tú?*" With no answer and heavy with sleep, she went back to dreaming.

In the morning, I woke up confident my abuelita had visited the altar both Paloma and I had set up for her the night before. I sat on my bed recollecting my dream then rose to my feet and stared out the window. I had dreamt I was walking. No, I was floating like la Llorona but wasn't sure if the woman in my dream was Abuelita Aurora, a bruja, or la Llorona.

It was November—in the time of . . . "*Ay de mí, Llorona Llorona, Llorona, llévame al río. Tápame con tu rebozo, Llorona, porque me muero de frío*".

On Top of a Treetop

Whirlwinds of muffled sounds came from their chainsaws shearing at the long branches of the barren mulberry treetops. Piled on top of each other, the dry branches spread across the dirt like fallen soldiers. These were the trees and branches of well-to-do folk Mother had once worked for on Saturday mornings. What had looked like blazing matches surrounding the Rancho Bernardo Estates—long after the trees were heavy with sweet white mulberries—were now skeletons with signs of a biting winter well on its way.

For Julian's father, Don Cipriano, our neighbor, with twenty years of tree trimming experience, climbing trees required less effort for balancing himself on top of treetops. And although Don Cipriano had faith in his old chainsaw and knew El Chango would never fail him on the job, he warned Julianito, his amateur son. "Cuidado con *El Chango* muchacho. Es muy traicionero. No te confíes. Un minuto piensas que estás seguro y el otro—pácatelas te agarra el chamuco," Don Cipriano assured his son, who looked closely at the chainsaw's chipped paint and closer at El Chango's jagged teeth.

That's what Julianito needed to remember: life on top of treetops was dangerous. And he had heard his uncle's stories—of falls, concussions, and broken bones that required a hospital visit or two—and even death—equivalent to thousands of dollars no family of six could ever afford.

Julian, wearing his steel-toe boots, should have worn spurs the day before Christmas. But trimming for fancy houses couldn't wait. On an outstretched mulberry's arm, stood Julian's meager body doing the job of his Uncle Alfredo, our neighbor, who was well in his late twenties. On top of a treetop, thinking about what his hard-earned money would buy, Julian imagined the crisp dollars running through his fingers, knowing he could now afford a gift for his María.

After a precarious step, Julian fumbled with the chainsaw, and that's when El Chango gnawed deep. With the sight of white flesh exposed, Julian toppled off the mulberry tree like a lifeless rag doll falling from a treehouse, and his warm blood seeped into the thirsty dirt. "¡Chacho pendejo! What did you do?" Don Cipriano screamed as he rushed to his Julianito.

Don Cipriano, with his fists clenched on the steering wheel, pressed on the gas as he drove off in his 1959 Chevy Apache truck. Fastened and asleep, Don Cipriano's fainted son didn't moan nor showed signs of pain.

Bewildered, Julianito woke up forty miles past Rancho Bernardo's local hospital and past nowhere near our neighborhood, across the border on a metal table, where it looked like a hospital—but smaller and contained the sounds of barking dogs.

Helena's Frijoles de la Olla

When Mom wasn't sewing and tending her dream garden, she cooked and cleaned. Mother loved beans. Every week at the dinner table she cleaned and sorted pinto beans, separating the broken beans from the whole ones. Patiently, she removed shriveled pinto beans and small lumps of dirt as she placed the good beans in her mint green colander. Standing in front of the running faucet, Mother's large brown hands rinsed the mound of beans carefully as if she were bathing a newborn baby. She'd stare out the kitchen window and with her butterfly gaze admire the rows of thorny rose bushes. Her eyes moved from the deep red to the blood orange and white roses she had planted with her own hands in our front yard as traffic slugged by.

While she drained the pinto beans, she looked for her hand-painted clay pot with creamy colored flower swirls. She poured the beans in the pot, added hot water, a wedge of onion and garlic, and brought it to a boil. After the foam rose, the kitchen became heavy with moisture from the steam coming from the pot of beans. She then skimmed the foam from the bean broth and lowered the flame. During the last cooking phase, Mother added salt. She then became a whirlwind tidying up our home as Mother swept, mopped the kitchen floor, and vacuumed the living room.

Two hours later, red, white and green decorated Mother's aqua blue talavera bowl of simmered pinto beans. Neatly diced tomato, onion, and cilantro floated in brownness. Heavy with the smell of cooked beans lingering in the kitchen, she'd take a slice of queso ranchero and roll it into a warm corn tortilla. With every spoonful of broth, she recollected stories of pinto beans.

Mother swooned and savored childhood memories confessing, "Mija, when my father died, frijolitos de la olla and tortillas were the only food my mother could feed us," she said as she closed her eyes and inhaled the steam from her bowl of frijolitos.

"Amá, you mean Abuelita Aurora?"

"Yes, Mija."

"When your Abuelo Fortino died, your Abuelita followed as if she died of heartache. We only had a handful of beans, and I gave my little brother and sister, your Uncle David and Madrina Cleo, bean broth for dinner."

"Amá, tell me about your family and the rancho."

"When my abuelito was a young boy, he helped build the rancho's stone fences—fences that corralled horses, chickens, hogs, and goats. Mija, we had everything—fruit trees, animals, and a beautiful lake. After a long day, our horses drank water from our small lake. Once it even rained silver fish at the lake."

"Really Amá? *It rained fish?*"

"Yes, Mija. When you talk to the winds, they listen. At the ranch, dogs ran in packs, chased passersby, and barked at spirits. Our small rancho in Michoacán, housed about thirteen families, Rancho San Juan de Ulúa, where everybody called each other uncle, aunt, and cousin. We all greeted each other and looked out for one another as if we were one big family, and we were, Mija. We were."

"Amá, that's why we called Tío El Gordo *uncle* when we lived in Idaho even though we weren't blood related?"

"Sí, Mija."

During hard times or not, my mother fed us pinto beans, tortillas, calabacitas, and stories. That's what she fed Uncle David and Madrina Cleo, and what our ancestors who had come before my mother had fed her. Simmered beans were the color of my mother's skin. I imagined Aurora, my abuelita, had been the color of dark creamy pinto beans all year around during spring, summer, fall, and winter. Raw pinto beans were freckled like my face—a sign of the past.

Mom says not to write recipes—to remember. I write them down in my scrapbook next to important news article clippings like "Rancho Peñasquitos Teenagers Attack Migrants" to never forget.

Helena's Frijoles de la Olla

1 Mexican clay pot filled with water
1 Mexican wooden spoon
7 handfuls of pinto beans
½ white onion
1 clove of garlic
Several pinches of salt
Lots of cariño and patience

Boil beans until tender and remember stories of frijolitos.

La Tamalera

A week prior to the tamalada, Mom bought chiles guajillo from across the border at the open market, El Mercado Hidalgo, in Tijuana because she wanted our tamales to taste like México. A day before the tamalada, chiles guajillo covered our family's dinner table, where photographs of cousins, extended family, and turquoise, yellow, and deep red silk roses peered through a clear plastic table cover. Our hands, drenched in cooking oil, destemmed, removed seeds, and veins from chiles. From the stove's burner, the smell of roasted guajillo rose, tickling my throat and nose. Sitting there in the company of my mother's comadres and friends, I imagined myself among the women elders of times past grinding dried chiles, garlic, and spices on their metates, producing a blend that made people swoon and mouths water for a tamal.

Had the tamales been prepared during Abuelita's time, Abuelito Pancho would have selected the best corn husks from his corn field for Abuelita Chucha. True tamaleras like my grandmother prepared tamales before the sun reached its splendor. Some modern tamaleras wore gloves and started rather late at about midday. We went through the prepackaged bags of corn husks, looking for the long and wide ones, so the masa would spread evenly on the husk. Unlike past times, nowadays tamales required two to three husks to hold the masa and meat in place.

The year Amá got a migraine Paloma became our family's official tamalera—a true leader with a strong pair of arms, like Abuelita Chucha had passed down to Father and Paloma. *Not me.* I couldn't understand what made gringos so crazy about tamales. My high school English teacher, Mrs. Wales, surprised me one day when she asked me, "Sofía, does your mother know how to make tamales?" I nodded with a silent yes. "Tell your mother I will pay her to teach me how to make tamales," Mrs. Wales offered eagerly. (Mom never taught Mrs. Wales because she moved up north before the end of the school year.)

What Mrs. Wales needed to know is a strong pair of arms kneaded the masa to produce quality tamales, like Abuela Chucha. During her times, women knelt in front of their metates using manos and physical strength to grind maize, producing cornmeal and then adding water, lard, and salt creating a thick, heavy masa. The modern Mexica leader, Paloma, however, made a phone call to our local Esperanza's Tortillería in Escondido and ordered thirty pounds of yellow masa for tamales. We no longer did the laborious kneading our ancestors had once done, but we acted like it required hard work.

"How does it look?"

"It needs more kneading. Don't you think?"

"Ándale pues. Ahora sigo yo."

After an hour of kneading masa, more like playing with Play-Doh, the ultimate Abuelita Chucha test required a full glass of water. Dad would take a small ball of dough and drop it into the glass. If the masa fell to the bottom, that meant it wasn't ready and required more kneading. If the small ball of dough rose to the top, the masa was ready for spreading on corn husks.

Corn husks, past and present, required the removal of its reddish-brown hair and soaking in lukewarm water to make their rough texture limp and manageable. With corn husks resting on our palms, as if we were looking at tepees, patiently we spread masa with a large silver spoon or wooden spoons on the bottom half of the husks. (From the land of Tlapehuala, Guerrero, at my friend Irma's house across the street, the spreading was done with their fingers in the shape of a chicken's head as their fingers pecked and spread the dough into place.) Like a swaddled baby, we carefully took the sides of the husk, folded one side over the other and then fastened the tamal with a tuck, leaving an end exposed like a baby's face.

Hours later, after Paloma stacked tamales standing up in Amá's large pot with very little water, for two hours the steam did its ancestral magic. I remembered the tamale joke at school.

"What do Mexican children unwrap for Christmas? Tamales since Mexicans can't afford presents."

Why would a Mexican child want to unwrap a tamal as a Christmas gift?

In México, corn husks were used in everyday life, from painted corn husk dolls to colorful fans and from cattle feed to a fire starter. Corn husk with its invaluable uses was sacred to the people of corn. Aztec dancers raised corn husk in the air to praise the spirit of corn, Centeotl. The making of tamales I concluded, as our batch came to an end, required more than just several centuries.

Only the people of corn and bananas could have invented tamales and corundas because corn husks and banana leaves surrounded them. I would rather have eaten a corunda than a tamal anytime, but then again—I guess they were cousins. Tamales were geometric—shaped like rectangles, and corundas were shaped like triangles, stars, and rectangles. Corundas, wrapped in a green banana leaf, gave the masa a green yellowish color and the jocoque (we settled for salted sour cream diluted with milk) added a distinct taste, unlike tamales.

And just because, according to the encyclopedia, the Aztecs served tamales to the Spanish Conquistadores, it didn't mean they had invented tamales. I could understand a craze for pumpkin flower soup and tortillas as our mother prepared— but tamales didn't convince me. The more I thought about tamales made me realize Indigenous women like Abuelita Chucha and Abuelita Aurora had made tamales long before the Aztecs. How did one explain an entire continent that ate tamales, with each region adding its own distinct flavor and womanly creativity—like black bean tamales, like black mole tamales, like sweet pineapple tamales, like lima bean tamales, like cheese and jalapeño tamales, like rice tamales, like tamales tied at the end with a thin strip of corn husk tied like a bow in a woman's hair, like potato, and olive tamales? *The Aztecs conquered a region not an entire continent.*

Tamales, tamales, tamales. Too time consuming if you asked me and the rules needed to change if I would take part in next year's tamalada. Next year, the boys, including my little brother, Cruz, needed to show up with their fancy long sleeves rolled up. Those who didn't participate in the tamalada, the ones with their arms crossed and whiners like me, wouldn't be allowed to eat tamales. Boys weren't going to take up space in the living room warming up the sofa while they watched a game of football, basketball, or fútbol. If I were La Tamalera, we would all face each other—remembering our grandparents through their stories. That's what we would do with our hands at next year's tamalada with the tamaleras and tamaleros, leading the way like our ancestors since ancient times.

Kissing Dreams from a Distance

The day we had been planning for years had finally arrived. Amá and Apá had saved enough money from mom's sewing and tanda, and with that money, the day of our trip to Michoacán, the place I had heard about through my parents' memories, would be a reality because Mom and Dad had purchased plane tickets to México.

But was M i c h o a c á n as magical and beautiful as Mom and Dad remembered?

Our red-eye flight, scheduled for 12:45 AM, vuelo tecolote, from the Tijuana International Airport, was in those days, the cheapest way a family of five could fly. Dad had made it very clear: "Paloma and Chofi, don't even think I'm going to help you carry your luggage, so only take what you need," but Paloma and I didn't listen. Convinced our father would carry our luggage, we stuffed our suitcases like big, fat, chubby tamales with lots of masa and very little meat and sauce.

During arrivals, fingers wavered in the air and tasseled sombreros swung like smoke signals beckoning relatives. Similar to our family, some mexicanos shook hands and hugged tightly. Some travelers' luggage consisted of cardboard boxes tied down with rope. I imagined the content of those boxes: brown cajeta for the sweet tooth, hand embroidered doilies with bright blue, green, bright pink, and orange flowers for all the comadres, including gifts for the neighbors, souvenir cups with the town's name engraved, a carved wooden toy, and a slingshot for nieces and nephews who were glued to the TV. But since those boxes didn't belong to me, my wandering eyes and satellite ears moved on. The main lobby was the perfect place to eavesdrop and pick up threads of conversations since I spoke and understood Spanish.

"El número de teléfono que me dio el compadre no sirve."

"Mira, qué grandote y chulo estás. Te pareces a tu papá. Déjame darte un abrazote."

"La cosa se puso cabrona en el pueblo."

"¿A cuánto le va a salir el coyote?"

"Espero que te haiga gustado el regalito que te traje."

Beyond my nearsighted vision in the far-off distance about a hundred feet away amidst the busy crowd stood a blurry silhouette wearing a black cowboy hat, a trench coat, jeans, and boots. I elbowed Paloma, directing my eyes in his direction, and she seconded with a nod.

After an hour of reading people, we finally boarded our From Guadalajara to Morelia, Michoacán, a glittery burgundy bus like the lowrider cars back home spearheaded to our father's homeland as an altar of saints glued to the dashboard guided our way. Nauseated from the strawberry-scented air freshener, I was glad when we finally arrived at our destination, Los Reyes, Michoacán, my father's birthplace, Callejón Rubén Romero #13, Colonia Santa Rosa, Los Reyes, Michoacán, México—the address on sealed envelopes. My father's Callejón de los Milagros.

Los Reyes is where Abuela Chucha took my father for dead. Predicting another stillborn, she placed him in a wooden crate.

My great-grandmother, a midwife, inspected her grandchild and asked, "What are you doing? This one is alive!" Abuela Chucha was happy with her Panchito, my father. Her mother-in-law, however, despised her grandchildren, because although they were wrapped in her white Castillo skin, all her children were damned with a round face and a flat nose like her daughter-in-law's. Los Reyes, that's where my father scavenged for the butcher's throwaway chicken scraps. Los Reyes was the place from where Father received long distance phone calls at East Los Angeles Street leaving him restless for hours until he spread his wings and began his journey to Michoacán.

We arrived in a taxi at Callejón Rubén Romero. The alley looked like an explosion of colors and smelled like wood burning and tortillas on a comal. While Father complained about the unpaved alley, Paloma and I sighed because our father kept his word: "I told you I wasn't going to help. ¡Ahora se chingan!"

At our Abuelo's doorstep, we slipped in through the wide wooden doors. Exhausted from dragging our luggage from airports to bus stations and walking on uneven sidewalks, we fell into a deep sleep on what we took for his bed—a hard wooden-framed bed radiating with a colorful sarape. Hours later at dusk we woke up itching and scratching from fleas feasting on visitors' blood. With a black shawl over her shoulder, Tía "La Güera," a fiery redhead, walked in, laughed and told us, "Your Abuelo's dog sleeps there." But Spanish had a multilayered dark comical twist: "El perro de tu abuelo se duerme allí."

That evening we left for the fair with all our cousins. One street after another Paloma and I pushed the weight of our bodies back as if we had clumsy horses' feet, learning to walk downhill through a labyrinth of pebbled and cement roads. At the fair, churros, corn, panqueques, chepos, and tortas teased our nose. Smells alone were enough to make me understand my father's nostalgia and his dream to return to his beloved hometown, Los Reyes, with our entire family. Walking arm in arm and holding hands with our girl cousins, elbow to elbow in a constant flow of people, in front of the Ferris wheel my cheeks went red because there stood a most memorable sight—the Mexican cowboy in his cowboy boots and cinto piteado—like mine.

The next day at Plaza Santa Rosa, surrounded by two-story colonial buildings and a cathedral, the branches of trees older than my father embraced visitors with their shade. Pensive and alone, sitting on a bench, I saw the cowboy, and this time our eyes locked. He stood and greeted me.

"Hola. ¿De dónde eres?"

"Nací en Valle del Sol."

"¿*Valle del Sol?* ¿Dónde queda ese lugar?"

"Nací en Los Ángeles, Alta California."

"Es mentira. No te creo."

We left the plaza and promised to meet at the tianguis, the local swap meet. But the tianguis, a long, long street didn't have a .75¢ entrance fee like the Oceanside or Escondido Swap Meet. Inevitably, we never found each other in the constant flow of people and never saw each other again.

The Mexican cowboy, however, taught me an important lesson. There was something about me that deceived the natives: I passed for a Mexican because my tongue moved freely. Where I came from, not all children of Mexican parents spoke Spanish.

México, where Amá and Apá were born, was difficult to let go because I recognized myself—my parents' muchacha, who appreciated the familiar tastes and sounds of the locals.

I wasn't the teenager at school who wore a gold necklace with the 100% Mexican medallion, marking genealogy and territory. My hair, my eyes, my nose, my lips, my teeth, my skin made *me*—Chofi. Sofía Martínez y con acentos. I couldn't hide my cheek bones and mouth. Boys tried to convince me I had kissing lips, *but they didn't fool me*. Dad had told me all about boys' mañas.

In a place, I had only imagined through my parents' stories, I was finally able to walk in my parents' dream—to visit Michoacán as a family. The x in México sounded comforting like a warm blanket—like the j in cobija—not like the ugly English pronunciation of Mex-see-coh. I took in my surroundings— the beauty of Mexican people, lakes, and waterfalls. Similar sounding, Michoacán like Michigan was a place of lakes, where I saw my brownness reflected. In Los Reyes, Michoacán, I looked at a mirror, where I swam with beautiful Indigenous and mestizo faces of all colors—some michoacanos were as dark as mole negro and others as light as flour tortillas. With an echo, syllables coming from my tongue reverberated in the waters of Michoacán's Los Chorros del Varal, Uruapán's waterfalls, Janitizio's Lake Pátzcuaro, and Camécuaro's National Lake. Staring at trees and lakes taught me to listen to myself— that no one could take my water and wind woman's faith away. No one.

I was butterfly kissing my parents' dream, and it was as sweet as a mother's kiss. I knew their dreams were my dreams like the words that escaped my mouth. On land, our family treaded like the ancient jaguar outside of enclosed grasslands. In waters, we were like sea turtles, migrating the oceans as we embarked on our journeys with our dreams in motion. Kissing dreams from a distance, my parents, like sea turtles, returned to the precise place of their birth. In the Michoacán skies, we were monarch butterflies, defying distances, fluttering with joy—feeling free.

Something Sacred

In Los Reyes, Abuelo's voice raspy from old age soothed my ears. I met Abuelo Francisco for the first time at his ninety-years-old, and he made physical work look effortless. I could see where my Mexican father had inherited his strong work ethic and superhuman strength.

Amused at my naivety and lack of basic survival skills, Abuelo Francisco chuckled when he caught me trying to cut a picket to heat water. With his sugarcane machete, I kept aiming at the center of the picket as if I were using an axe. "A ver, Hija, dame acá," Abuelito requested as he took the machete and picket from my clumsy hands. Holding the picket straight up, Abuelo gave it two taps at one end and made a small wedge. Once the machete lodged in, he dropped his arm and the picket split in half. "Gracias Abuelito Francisco," I responded as he handed me the wood. Chuckling at me, he went on with his laborious day.

With his suspenders over his shoulders, red T-shirt and brown checkered pants, Abuelito, in his nineties, reminded me of Rocky Balboa's trainer—lean and strong for his age. In the United States, my abuelo, a former bracero, had been sprayed with DDT, and it made me cry inside to think my grandfather had been treated like a cockroach in my country, the land of the free. Father once told me how Abuelo had returned to Michoacán, land of the monarch butterfly, with broken wings—wounded and in crutches carrying a Gas and Electric military radio. After that, he never talked about the U.S. or returned to El Norte—not even to visit his grandchildren.

During our visit, every day when he walked to Plaza Santa Rosa, his dog, Chicle, Paloma, and I tagged along but couldn't keep up with Abuelo's fast pace as he easily lifted his legs to walk on high sidewalks (a sign of Los Reyes's heavy rains). When Abuelito returned from Plaza Santa Rosa, he sat at his doorstep on his green wooden chair with its seat made of rope. With his leathery fingers, Abuelito Pancho removed dry maize from cobs to sell and to store them to heat water.

When Abuela Chucha died, Abuelito learned to make his own flour tortillas. Women younger than Abuelo Francisco circled him like crows, but Abuelo wanted to be alone with his corn field, his thoughts, and his companion, Chicle. Watching him while I dusted his plants in his red and green kitchen and swept his earthen floor, I observed how Abuelito's old hands glowed with warmth as he took a little handful of flour, sprinkled, and spread it on the table. Then, he placed a small ball of dough on a wooden table and patted it down with his floury fingertips. With his rolling pin, Abuelito shaped the dough into a large circle ready for stretching on his left palm and the heated comal.

The irresistible smell of homemade tortillas brought back memories of Dad teaching Paloma and me how to make flour tortillas on a small countertop in our small apartment in Vista. Abuelo stood next to his small stove and turned the tortilla several times as he waited for the tortilla to rise and the brown spots to darken. Staring at my grandfather, I remembered Dad saying Abuelo looked like Anthony Quinn in his youth with his long-chiseled face; I could see there were still remnants of his bracero days in his old man's body. After the tortilla cooled off, he gave me a flour tortilla he had just made with his very own hands. In exchange, I handed him a plastic rosary I found tucked between a row of jars. We smiled at each other. There was something sacred in our silence.

Distance, time, and money had robbed Paloma, Cruz, and me of a grandfather's stories, but Abuelo's face, voice, and leathery hands echoed in my memory with every bite of a Mexican flour tortilla—ever so present in the Californias—Baja California and Alta California.

In Michoacán, I had a grandfather who smelled like corn and flour. Abuelo's face was shaped like a huarache, and my face was shaped like a corn tortilla—like Abuelita Chucha's round face. In El Norte, we had been separated by a militarized American border, but we sure did share the same taste buds.

El Borracho

"So I remember when we were driving
Driving your car
Speed so fast it felt like I was drunk
City lights, lay out before us
And your arm felt nice wrapped around my shoulder and
I—I had a feeling that I belonged
I—I had a feeling I, could be someone, be someone,
be someone"
                    —Tracy Chapman, "Fast Car"

Drinking on a weekday and leaving behind empty cans of beer and bags of Doritos on the beige and worn-out Monte Carlo's tapestry, he hobbles side to side and then almost falls forward to reach the front doorstep of our house. On his way to the front door, he kneels and crouches forward as he citrifies the grass with vomit. Dad kneels down next to mother's crimson red, soft yellow, white and bright pink roses—lots of roses she sacrifices—offerings for a life-size replica of the very Virgencita de Guadalupe who always listens to her prayers silently to make the drinking go away. "Please Virgencita, I ask you with all my heart that Pancho not drink anymore. Yes, I know he is a hard worker, but look at the bad influence he's become on our daughters, Paloma and Sofía, and our son, Crucito. I also ask you to protect each one of our children with your sacred tilma. Thank you for listening to my prayers."

In those days, Dad was EL BORRACHO right out of La Lotería with lots of pictures to read. *"Ellll Borrachoooo,"* the cardholder called out. A lucky winner announced, *"¡Aquí! Buenas con El Borracho,"* as the winner claimed the jackpot of nickels and dimes, and all players cleared their pinto beans or pennies off their favorite card that brought them luck. But not so *buenas* for those who lived with an obnoxious, hot-tempered borracho like my father who now drank on weekdays and weekends and drove back drunk with Amá closing her eyes and praying to all her saints. She clenched her right hand on the unraveling stitches of the Monte Carlo's seat while we had enjoyed the roller coaster ride as children.

"Come on Dad! Go faster! Faster!"

"Girls, please do not talk to your father. Can't you see he's driving?"

One time Dad raced "a real pendejo" on the freeway—a cop. The police officer dropped off Crucito at home that time. Nothing changed after hours of A.A. meetings. The drinking continued. Some *borrachos sobered up on Mondays while working and, of course, always* denied they had a drinking problem. A drunk will always tell you he can cure a hangover if he drinks another beer, which does work, because he's in an endless drunken state of mind. A drunk will always claim he's perfectly healthy because he's numbing his pain.

Parties without beer, according to Dad, "Valían pura madre," so at fiestas where alcohol was prohibited, which were very few, he'd cut a Pepsi can with a knife, place it as a label on a Budweiser can, and sit like a king holding his latest invention while the mariachi played José Alfredo Jiménez's "El Rey":

"Con dinero y sin dinero

Yo hago siempre lo que quiero

Y mi palabra es la ley"

On weekdays, we knew better and remained behind walls and out of sight or else at 12:30 AM on a school night, Dad would call a meeting, where he always spoke the last word and demanded we listen to his hostile words. "Así que estas dos pendejitas van a tratar de decirme que estoy mal. Ya decía mi madre, 'Cría cuervos y te sacaran los ojos.'" The worst part about his drinking was having to bite my tongue because Mom always said, "Don't say anything. Stay quiet. Sofía, haven't you learned anything?"

Apá was a good man until the drinking spell began. For most of his life, our father had been not just a good man but a great man of kind acts and words. Although hot tempered, he was patient and taught us to box and stand our ground. He paid us money to learn how to make flour tortillas and for bringing home good grades. He taught us smoking cigarettes and drinking coffee were drugs and corrosive to the human body.

But when he started working his new construction job, hot summers with a 107° beating sun and winter winds whipping his face broke him. Beer took the edge off so much he forgot the meaning of family. And drinking blurred my father's vision, and so I began fearing his presence because his words cut deep. I wished El Borracho remained trapped in a playing card, not in my father. It was painful to watch Cruz with an Uncle David haircut grab Apá a can of beer when he asked for one and then another and another.

What could I do?

I was only his daughter and not even the eldest. My mother loved my father, and she would never leave him; instead, she kneeled, prayed, and would cure him with compassion, guava tea, and loving words. "Viejito, ya vente a dormir. Mañana tienes que trabajar temprano."

"Sofía, ¿qué soñaste?"

On Sunday mornings before Sunday mass, while tidying up the house, we talked about our dreams. We all eagerly shared our dreams with each other. For Paloma, Cruz, and I, it was important for Amá to hear and interpret our dreams.

"Sofía, ¿qué soñaste?" my mother asked curiously as she sprayed cleaner on the grout between the white tiles, and we cleaned the kitchen together.

"Amá, I dreamed about two finches. Two small finches with fully extended wings fluttered desperately. They were trying to escape from a large red cage with its doors wide open. But even though the two finches weren't hurt—nor did they have clipped wings, *they couldn't fly away*. In my dream, there was something standing in the background—but I couldn't tell what it was. I think it was a black shadow—," I recounted my dream as I degreased the wooden cabinets.

"Chofi, were the birds hungry? What did the water look like?" Amá asked as her pensive eyes locked with mine.

"The cage had plenty of seeds and clean water. The bottom of the cage was lined with clean newspaper. Nothing appeared to be missing. The finch that looked slightly smaller kept fluttering down as if it were fainting or dying. The other finch tried to help the fluttering one but couldn't do anything."

Amá then began her soothsaying and interpreted my dream. "Mija, people can be taken away from us—for many years. Other times *forever*. But we always manage to survive. Although we do need food and water, to be happy we need each other's human connection. Food and water are never enough. Sofía, what was standing in the background? What are you afraid of?"

What was I afraid of? I wasn't afraid of spirits like Abuelita Aurora. That's for sure. *But what was lurking in the background in my dream? What was I afraid of?* I kept asking myself. *What am I afraid of?*

I was terrified.

I was terrified of the principal's stories in elementary and high school, the news, and what the TV said could happen to girls and young women like me on TV shows and in movies.

Paloma and I could get abducted.

We could get slandered.

I could get raped like Lindsey.

I could get murdered, and nobody would ever find out who the killer was—or the honest truth. And lately, I feared our father's anger when he drank two six packs or more by himself.

But what could Paloma and I do?

A Woman's Body

Mexican commercials and the news didn't care. We'd be eating dinner with a mouthful of tortilla, beans, and green salsa, and sure enough, on my parents' big screen TV that took up half of the living room wall, we'd get bombarded with commercials, advertising antifungal treatments. And there in front of our eyes were the before and after close-up photos, showing the effectiveness of the wondrous products. Then, between commercials, on a weekday something unsettling on TV difficult to believe escaped the news reporter.

The unbelievable happened. Something that when I first heard I couldn't believe—something that sounded straight out of the yellow *¡Alarma!* magazines with gory photos of accidents and murders I had come across as a kid when we crossed the border to Tijuana and Mexicali—except this time it was on the Mexican news.

The human carcasses, including a pregnant body, had been found mutilated, tortured, strangled, raped, and disposed like battered old TVs, VCRs, and putrid refrigerators in the outskirts of Ciudad Juárez, Chihuahua, in empty lots, in sewage channels, in ditches, on roads, especially the road to Casas Grandes, in baseball fields but mostly in the city—anywhere that left someone alone, sick, and devouring a woman's body.

And who could that person or those people be?

And where were the men—the real men—who would never let this happen to their daughters, wives, and sobrinas?

According to the reporter, these deaths were growing in number. "Angélica Márquez Ledezma, 16; Sonia Ivette Ramírez, 13; Elizabeth Castro García, 17; Olga Alicia Carillo Pérez, 19; Silvia Helena Rivera Morales; Not Identified, 14–18; No Name Woman, approximately 30 . . . ." Some victims were students—usually with long hair. Others were killed in their own vicinities or were on their way or coming back from the maquiladoras—and sometimes looking for work. "Eighty-five percent of the factories are U.S. owned," continued the reporter.

Who were the companies that were making money and turning a blind eye? Bodies were being found like used bullet shells in the desert.

Women's bodies.

When I heard the Canal 12 de Tijuana news, I wanted to believe it was an error on the teleprompter. It had to have been an error because on the American news, I had heard about cat and dog food poisoning pets. But the newscaster had said very clearly MUJERES, not dogs, nor cats. *WOMEN.* I had never ever heard anything this disturbing on the news in English.

As the living room caved in on me and the TV screen transmitted warped images that would have never been shown on American news channels, what the TV announced was the lives of one hundred American dogs meant more than a Mexican woman's body. The lives of endangered animals caused riots among American pet owners and animal rights activists. When all along, we had always been an endangered species.

Was this part of the reason father had always been so strict and overprotective with us—his first and secondborn daughters?

Along the United States and Mexican border, resided Juárez, Chihuahua, and El Paso, Texas, where according to my government teacher's guest speaker, NAFTA would create more jobs for impoverished countries. Instead, my parents' news taught me the desert created a salted sea of mermaids, and their bodies were tangled in poachers' nets, with no country to run to, because some—not all—the women wore fishnet stockings.

Mexican news didn't cross the border. Because to Americans, the lives of Mexican women didn't mean a thing—no monetary value—and maybe their deaths would help keep women in their place.

These women hadn't enlisted in war, but every day they walked through minefields. Bodies popped up like rodents in a real Whack the Gopher game. Dead bodies didn't go away with a blow to the head, and burlap sacks only served to annoy foreign companies that didn't need the news spotlight. American companies wanted to stretch their money in México with no consequences or accountability.

Why bother—they were just Mexican women's bodies.

The Story of the First Year

In our backyard on a Sunday afternoon, finches flew from tree to tree as Tía Alicia and Amá sat surrounded by Spanish moss hanging from our apricot tree's branches. With her sharpest knife, Amá cleaned the nopales, removing the espinas with ease. The thorns fell on the newspaper she had placed on the grass. Underneath the tree's shade with her hands resting on her lap with a calmness that comes with age, Tía Alicia sang and shared her stories.

The Martínez Castillo had a way of telling stories. While we were growing up when she visited us, Tía Alicia's stories had always made us giggle and sometimes even cry. The story Dad's sister told us this time—she made it very clear—was about Paloma and my future. Taking a blade of grass to her mouth and in deep thought, Tía Alicia began the story of the first year. From where we sat on the grass, we stared at her large brown eyes and listened attentively as her eyes became wishing wells for her two young nieces.

"Paloma and Sofia, mis hijas, blood of my blood, my mother never warned me about marriage. Instead, your Abuela Chucha told me to carry my cross after my first beating. I can assure you the first year together will be the most important year of your lives since it will mark your destiny. I'm telling you this because I don't want the same thing that happened to me to happen to either of you.

The first year—if you wash all the dirty dishes day in day out—you will always wash them. Always. The first year, even if you fall ill, you will wash piles and piles of clothes. For the rest of your lives, you will never get a thank you for a single drop of sweat. Believe me, at first, he will be very angry, but with time, he will learn to wash for himself, because like any human being, he will need clean clothes. Let's say one day he washes your clothes and ruins your favorite blouse—don't complain. Say thank you, and teach him what his mother and father never taught him. If one day he decides to cook for you and the food isn't good, don't complain. Say encouraging words and teach him. Praise him. Tell him his cooking could use more spices or this or that the next time. One day, when you are no longer in his life, he will be grateful for making him the well-rounded man he became. Queridas sobrinas, Paloma and Sofia, learn to live a happy life—do not sacrifice your own happiness for a man. Both of you are still young. Let my story teach you both a lesson. These are the humble words I leave you with. Take my words, and remember them when the time comes. Do what you must do because in the end everything will be okay."

After the story of the first year, Mother looked at her sister-in-law and thanked her with a smile, and I wondered if Tía Alicia was going to die or if there was something I didn't know. *Why had Tía Alicia told us this story?* Tía Alicia and Amá stood up, straightened their long-ruffled skirts. They went inside to check up on the pot of beans, cook rice, and dice onions, tomatoes, and cut cilantro for the nopalitos we would be eating for dinner. Meanwhile, the men in our family sat and drank on tree trunks, played guitar, and sang while they collected empty Budweiser cans under the eucalyptus trees' shade. Next to the thick large Canary palm, Dad prepared the grill for a carne asada.

"Paloma, did Mom tell you something I don't know?"

"No, Sofía. Why do you ask?"

"I just thought it was strange to hear Tía Alicia warn us about marriage as if she could foretell the future."

Paloma and I lay on the grass in silence thinking about Tía Alicia's words and our future with our hands behind our heads looking up through the guayaba tree's branches at a washed-out blue sky with passing white nebulous clouds trailing behind and our homework due Monday morning.

The Night Paco Almost Had a Heart Attack

"Cucurrucucu, paloma
Cucurrucucu, no llores
Las piedras jamás, paloma
¡Qué van a saber de amores!
Cucurrucucu, cucurrucucu
Cucurrucucu, paloma, ya no llores"
 —Lola Beltrán, "Paloma negra"

The night before I had dreamt Paloma and Crucito crying, surrounded by sealed cardboard boxes. Against the cold-glass window, warm rain poured heavily as the boxes were getting wet and slowly unraveling. A Corona yellow covered de floor, and the red tape could no longer hold the boxes together. In the dream, we hold each other tight and are surrounded by feathers. On Paloma's forehead, a third eye she cannot see.

That night in the kitchen, the kettle was already boiling Mother's té de valeriana. Father's beer can fell, and yellow liquid dripped down the table. Dad was so drunk and mad as he stumbled in the kitchen that Paco started screaming.

"*Papá!—Paco*," I yelled nervously.

"*Paco qué? Look what I can do to this fuckin' parrot! Helena, calla este pinche perico.*"

171

Father opened Paco's black birdcage. When father's construction hands squeezed Paco violently, I thought Paco had died. His green feathers fluttered like a chicken, trying to escape as if she were being wrung by the neck. Wheezing for his last breath, Paco lay at the bottom of his cage not as a bird but like a fish flopped on his belly.

"I don't care about this fuckin' bird! ¡Mira! ¡Mira!" Dad screamed violently. I could tell he had been drinking because I couldn't recognize him. He had transformed into a rockhead at the bottom of the sea, and it was impossible to reach inside him. Without Dad noticing, I left him alone and angry in the kitchen.

In Paloma and my room, with my wings trampled by a man I had called father, I locked myself inside. I replayed Paco's screams. I was certain Paco had suffered a heart attack because I couldn't hear his screams or singing coming down the hall from the kitchen. Paco had lost his voice.

In my room, I screamed with all my might on paper recollecting dreams and stories, remembering our days in Los Ángeles, in Idaho, and in Vista . . . when Dad and Mom promised our dreams would come true if we worked hard.

And they did. *But what had happened to our family in El Norte?*

When Paloma arrived from work, she didn't escape Dad's foaming wrath either.

"¡Paloma! Why did you get home so late?"

"Dad—I."

"Don't interrupt me! If you don't like it, the door is wide open! You can leave!"

Paloma and I took Dad's words to heart. Hastily, attempting to escape our father's wrath, Paloma quickly walked to our room. As a deer caught in bright highlights, Paloma, my sister with the name of a bird, froze in our room's doorway.

"Paloma, grab a pair of underwear! ¡Vámonos Hermana!"

The night Paco almost had a heart attack Paloma and I left headfirst, zigzagging through the front door as we extended our wings and flapped mightily.

Listening to Dad's hollering screams, Cruz woke up. Into the darkness, we escaped a drunken man's iron birdcage we had called home. We left Cruz, holding onto Mom, and Paco behind. As our cooing mother lay in her empty nest, Cruz tried consoling our mother; she grieved all night as if her wings had been violently torn from her. With trails of tears behind us, we escaped a house, where lately we had been walking on eggshells.

The floor shook violently under our feet. We had been let loose. And the birdcager's imaginary door had always been wide open. We didn't know we were two Adelitas, two soldaderas, with limitless boundaries in a world of reconcilable differences, and Pancho Villa or our father wasn't here to stop us. Not a stranger's words, not a father's words, not a mother's silence, or a boss's words could tear or pluck our monarch wings. No one could stop us because we had been taught our visions for the future were where our dreams began. And like a young, sober father had once foreseen for his children's future, a pen filled with ideas was a necessary tool to paint dreams with paper, letters, and numbers, and we knew and never forgot we owed that to brilliant, illiterate minds. We needed to make room for our dreams because both Paloma and I knew our dreams were Amá and Apá's dreams, and their dreams were ours too.

Renegades

We were back in Vista—this time on the northside in the outskirts of the city by the nurseries. At her front door, Doña Paula, wearing a purple checkered apron, waited for us. By her feet, a little spotted dog wagged her tail and jumped up and down.

"Pásenle, muchachas. My niece called to tell me you were on your way. I was beginning to worry."

"Doña Paula, we're so sorry we're keeping you up this late—" Paloma apologized as her voice withered.

"Don't worry, muchachas. What matters is that you're both safe. I just finished watching my novela. Pintinta, ven pa' acá. Deja a las muchachas en paz." Her eyes squinted as she glanced at her clock and her dog. "Siéntense en el sofá, muchachas."

I wondered if Paloma was hungry too because Doña Paula's apartment smelled like tacos de papa, and my pansa was starting to growl. In her living room, dolls were neatly lined up on a shelf mounted on the wall. From where I sat, I could see a sewing basket with a tortilla napkin with yellow and turquoise flowers on a wooden hoop, a remote control, and reading glasses. Sitting next to me, I could see Paloma's eyes looked as if she had an allergic reaction. Swollen. I put my arm around my sister to comfort her.

"Muchachas, vamos a la cocina. Seguro que tienen hambre."

"Doña Paula, por favor, no se moleste."

"¿Cómo que no? Vengan." Doña Paula with great big arms of a luchadora led Paloma and me to her kitchen.

"Doña Paula, thank you so much for taking us in. We'll call my mom tomorrow. This incident caught us off guard. We didn't know what to do, so we ran to our car and called up your niece. She didn't think it was a good idea for us to stay—even if it was across the street."

"Muchachas, we can talk tomorrow. No se preocupen."

"Doña Paula, did your niece tell you my sister and I go to college and work. We're not planning on missing any classes. We're getting ready for our finals."

"Yes, Irmita, did tell me that. Don't worry. You can stay here until you find another place. My roommate left for Honduras. She'll be back in two weeks. Pintita and I could use the company in the meantime. When she gets back, we'll make room for all of us. Hasta en el piso se pueden dormir."

"Thank you, Doña Paula."

"Doña Paula, I have a question for you."

"A ver, muchacha, pregúntame."

"When you were a little girl did you have dolls?" I asked as she grabbed napkins for us.

"When I was a little girl, my parents couldn't afford toys. One day on my birthday my mom surprised me with a doll she made from a flour sack. Ay, mi mamita chula. Como la extraño. Pintita, ya te di de comer. Hazte pa' allá sino te voy a sacar al patio."

"Oh, that makes sense," I said as I glanced at the wall, "So now that you're older, with the money you earn, you buy as many dolls as you wish?"

"Ay muchacha, I've never thought about that. It's possible. They keep me company. My children live up north in Merced and Sacramento; ya se me casaron todos. ¿Les gustaron los tacos? Híjole, se me olvidó el quesito."

Doña Paula's tacos were incredibly delicious, and her salsa roja was perfect—not bland nor too salty.

"Sí, Doña Paula, que ricos están sus tacos."

"Y también su salsa de molcajete," I added.

"Gracias muchachas. Es secreto de familia," Doña Paula winked her left eye, and her smile widened. "Pero a lo mejor les puedo compartir mi receta. Se llaman tacos de canasta. Tienen su chiste. Eh. Bueno muchachas, let's clear up the table, so I can find you clean cobijas. On weekdays, I wake up at five o'clock in the morning to get ready to cook and pack up my lunch. I hope I don't make too much noise in the kitchen."

"Don't mind us. We don't know how to pay you back for this huge favor. We didn't have anywhere to go."

"We can talk more tomorrow. Get some rest. You've had a rough night. I've been there too. I left my husband and ran away with my three children. Antes de que se duerman, las voy a barrer para que descansen."

In the Place of Books

Away from home, we regained our strength as we learned to walk for the first time on our own two feet. On campus, I could forget about Dad's grudge for leaving the house (even though he was the one who kicked Paloma out, and I followed). After the heartache he put us through, Dad couldn't deny we were his Rocky Girls.

Like Abuela Chucha, I'm calling my father back because he's worth our Abuela's love medicine. I don't look for cross streets like my grandmother. I just close my eyes, imagine my father, and call him back with my thoughts.

Apáááá.

Apáááá.

Apáááá.

Apáááá.

Because of Dad, I felt safe at school since he taught me to keep boys with bad intentions at a distance and stay focused on the college path. And he taught me to strike back—if necessary—with my closed fists or anything within reach.

After my health class on my way to the restroom, Rico, a guy in one of my classes, asked, "Aren't you afraid?" as he stared at me. I replied with a question, "Afraid of *what?*"

"Those books," he pointed at a psychology textbook, an anthology of literature, and two novels I carried under my arm. I stared down at my books, but I didn't see hissing snakes, trying to bite my hand. "No. Not at all. I just have to read the books—make sense of the words on the pages." I answered with a smirk and a chuckle as I walked to the parking lot.

Rico headed to his next class, and I kept thinking about his question on my drive to Doña Paula's, our temporary living space for a few more weeks: "Aren't you afraid?" *Was I supposed to be afraid of books? Was Rico afraid of books? Were people afraid of books?* The books I carried under my arm compiled stories just like Amá and Apá's stories. In Psychology 101 and Professor Gawomone's literature class, we interpreted signs and symbols just like my mother interpreted our dreams. Reading and writing didn't scare me either. College, the place of books, wasn't scary at all. Spirits I dreamed didn't scare me—not the ghost type like Abuelita Aurora but, yes, the drinking type because I had witnessed Dad's transformation from a kind-hearted father, although overprotective, to an angry totalitarian, imagining evil spirits.

Since Professor Gawomone read my work to his colleagues and I had done well in English classes, I took it as a sign and signed up for journalism for the summer. *Why not?* If I could write for a college English class, I could write for Journalism 101 and write stories for the school newspaper. I was hungry for stories—hungry for telling stories and looked forward to my first day of summer classes.

As soon as I got home, I called Mom to share important news. I twirled the phone's extension cord between my fingers while waiting for Mom to pick up the phone.

"Hola. ¿Quién habla?" I heard my mother's familiar voice and Paco's singing in the background.

"Amá, it's me Sofía. ¿Cómo está? Is Dad still angry at Paloma and me?"

"I'm feeling better, Mija. Yes, you know your father."

"Okay Amá. I have something to share with you."

"¿Qué paso, Mija? Ay Mija. *Are you pregnant?*"

"No Amá! Why would you ask me that? I want to tell you something very important. I decided on my major—*J O U R N A L I S M*. I'm starting my first journalism class next week!"

"Journalism. ¡Qué bueno, Mija! *Will it make you happy, Sofía?*"

"I think so, Amá."

On the phone, I smiled like a Martínez Ramírez even though mom couldn't see my face beaming with joy.

"Que bueno, Chofi. As you have learned, writing comes with responsibility. *Remember when Irma and you protested at St. Mark's?* Readers weren't happy about the protest or the article in the *San Diego Times*. And even though Father Diego had to leave, the church made sure it replaced him with a bilingual priest, who spoke Spanish."

"I know, Amá. You were so embarrassed when you and your comadres found out about the article in the newspaper. But haven't you and Dad always taught Paloma and me to tell the truth? *Isn't journalism the same?*"

"Sí, Sofía, you're right. Being a liar and an hablador isn't good. Como dice el refrán, 'Al que obra mal, se le pudre el tamal.' I don't know if you remember, but your Dad had a cousin who was studying to be a journalist in Mexico City."

"*Really Amá?*" My eyes brightened with the news. *Why couldn't I remember this important detail?*

"Yes, he was one of the students assassinated in La Matanza de Tlatelolco."

"Oh my God, Amá! *I can't believe what you're telling me.*"

"Your uncle attended UNAM in Mexico City. La Universidad Nacional Autónoma de México. Miguel Martínez Solorio—that was his name. Your father's cousin. Do you remember his picture?"

"I do, Amá! He's the one with the Superman curl. I remember the small black and white photo shaped like an oval in our burgundy family album! I might even look into writing in Spanish like my uncle for UCSD's *Voz Fronteriza* Professor Gawomone mentioned during his office hours. There are a bunch of writers like me. I just need to look for them."

"Mija, let me look for your uncle's photograph in our album."

"Please do, Amá!"

I wanted to know everything about Tío Miguel, especially now I knew someone in our family had studied journalism in México.

"Sofía, did you and Paloma sit down with José Armando to sign the paperwork?"

"We're signing the loan documents tomorrow, Amá. Don't worry. Okay Amá. I have to head to work now. Say hi to Cruz, and give him a big hug for me. Te quiero mucho, Amá. ¡Nos vemos pronto!"

"Yo también, Mija. Échale muchas ganas, Sofía. Tú puedes, Mija! Remember to take a nap if you get tired and drink water before you go to sleep. Salúdame a Doña Paula."

"Okay, Amá! I'm drinking more water. I swear."

By Sofía Martínez

On my first day of summer school, eagerly waiting for my first journalism class to start, I looked around. Like most of my English classes, one or two brown faces sat in the class, including myself. This class struck me different from other classes when Professor Marshall, a redhead wearing a blue beret, walked into class with a police officer. Professor Marshall was a woman, and she was Black.

"Good morning class. Welcome. I'm Professor Ida Marshall from Lansing, Michigan, and I'll be teaching your Journalism 101 class this summer. Unfortunately, I received a death threat over an article I wrote a week ago, so campus police will be in the classroom for the day," Professor Marshall informed our class. Several students gasped, including myself, but we all knew we wanted to learn to write stories, so of course, we stayed in her class.

Since our first assignment was due the following Thursday, Professor Marshall taught us the nuts and bolts to write a good article within the first week of class. I couldn't wait to write my first article, so I could point to "By Sofía Martínez," written in bold to show Mom and Dad. Even if Dad was still mad, I knew he would be proud of me. How I wished I could add Ramírez after Martínez to give credit to my mother's family lineage. During Professor Marshall's lecture, I wondered if I should write a film review, a sports column, or a feature story. I had to decide and fast because writing for a newspaper required writing under pressure, and I needed to divide my time between Sandwich Alley and schoolwork to pay the bills.

The following day, when Professor Marshall asked for our topics for the upcoming newspaper publication, I quickly raised my hand high to pitch my topic—the mural controversy. The mural was a big deal; it was important for people like me to see ourselves reflected at our campus like the great master, Diego Rivera, had done in México for the people. *Why couldn't a mural be painted by the entrance at our college?* I had seen murals in Los Ángeles and Barrio Logan painted by Chicanas and Chicanos with colors as bright as sarapes and piñatas, telling people—like me—we belonged. We have been here. People from up north from the Fresno area and down south travelled to see and celebrate our heritage rooted in resistance, danza, music, and floricanto every April on Chicano Park Day in Barrio Logan. Judy Baca's *The Great Wall of Los Angeles* mural, a former flood control channel, depicted the images of Indigenous people of the land, Pío Pico, Bridge "Biddy" Mason, Chinese workers, and everyone who fabricated our existence in Alta California and beyond.

At Chicano Park, gigantic working bodies like Amá and Apá's held picks, shovels, and torches; they stood proudly holding up the Coronado Bridge with their superhuman strength. For Mexicans and Chicanos, murals were like books, but instead visitors could see with their own eyes how actions unfolded into the people's version of their stories—not as footnotes or brief paragraphs in history books. Murals even inspired onlookers to imagine future generations coming together—at the human level—as one people from different backgrounds with tribal headdresses and fancy hats to sombreros and top hats.

Luckily for me, Professor Marshall accepted my topic. According to Professor Marshall, the censor never won. In Journalism 101, I learned I had my personal opinions, but I needed to be impartial as a journalist and never present fabricated lies or fallacies to the reader. With the tools of a journalist—a small yellow notepad, a tape recorder, and a blue ballpoint pen in hand, and most importantly—my ethical mind—I was ready to book appointments, to stop by offices, to make a few phone calls, and to ask questions.

By the following day, I learned the college was renovating the campus and wanted to go with *a modern look*—mural free. But I didn't believe that story since I had visited El Palacio de Bellas Artes in Mexico City during our trip to México. According to the Chicana muralist, Patricia Frida Izquierdo Aguayo, "La Dreamer" the college president told her the mural project did not suit the college's modern architecture and the campus already had a gallery. I interviewed professors and students too, and they all agreed the college needed to represent them, by depicting the community's accomplishments and struggles since the college had been listed as a Hispanic Serving Institute even though I didn't see any Chicanos or Latinos in my new-found major.

"Textbooks focus on information that don't represent our true history and voices. A mural at the college will validate our existence, and more Chicanitas and Chicanitos will see themselves reflected and will want to attend college," Alicia, a tall Chicana, with black eyeliner and hoop earrings, wearing a M.E.Ch.A shirt, told me as I quickly wrote notes for my first article.

I learned our college could afford a mural, and with enough signatures, students could present the project to the Board of Trustees—the mural could one day be a reality. Because without students, there'd be no college.

I could write about that.

And then I wondered what a mural about San Marcos would look like. How had San Marcos received its Spanish name? But that's another story . . .

Dream Makers

Tía Alicia was right. And Amá was right too. Everything will be okay. We took Amá's lead. If Paloma and I combined our income, we could afford a house of our own—even if it's small.

Before moving into our casita, Amá opened all the windows and Doña Paula, holding an abalone shell with copal and sacred feathers in her right hand, cleared and blessed all the rooms. Amá joined Doña Paula with prayer; she blessed herself and then sprinkled holy water in all the corners of our bedrooms and living room. With the smoke guiding her through the house, Doña Paula entered the spirit world. In her embroidered dress and her rebozo wrapped around her, Doña Paula made room for us as she walked through our new home, making sure she didn't miss any space as she mediated and chanted for our safety and wellbeing.

This is your sacred home.

You are safe in your home.

Love and protect your home.

Flowers will always bloom in your home.

Fear and anger will not enter your home.

Your Spirits will always be with you and guide you.

With Ama and Doña Paula's blessings, we are one with our new casita.

Across the street, the neighbor, who lives in front of us, ignores us and acts like we don't exist. She never says hello, but her husband does. But it doesn't matter because we have a bigger family. The Oceanside beach is close to our little Spanish style house, surrounded with pink and orange geraniums in pots and Doña Paula and our Amá's medicinal plants to cure all sorts of ailments. We have to stay healthy and strong because we work and go to school to pay our bills.

In our new sanctuary on Flame Tree Street, Paloma and I reign over the household. At our very own place, there are no planchas or ironing boards. Every morning I tip my hat at all the flowers in our garden of dreams and photographs of Abuelita Aurora and Abuelita Chucha we placed by our little house's entrance. A pot of black beans cooks on a low flame. We sweep, we mop, we cook, we plant seeds, and most importantly, we stay up studying because we are going to college as our father and mother had always dreamed.

Paloma is still thinking about numbers; she wants to be an accountant, and one day she wants to run her own Paloma Martínez Foundation for smart boys and girls, so they learn to love numbers like her. For sure I don't want to be a kindergarten teacher after all. I want to be like Tía Alicia Martínez and my family, a storyteller—but for the *San Diego Times*—because there are important stories left out of our times. I want to fulfill Tío Miguel Martínez Solorio's dream—to become a journalist and report with the eyes and ears of an ethical reporter.

In my Introduction to Chicano Studies class, I learned a Mexican-American, a Chicano journalist, wrote for the *Los Angeles Times* in the 60s. R u b é n S a l a z a r. But when Rubén Salazar reported on the Vietnam War's National Chicano Moratorium, a deputy sheriff tragically killed Rubén Salazar when the officer threw tear gas while he sat at a bar. If Rubén Salazar, someone of Mexican heritage and brown *like me*, could be a journalist, I can be a journalist too—even if it's dangerous to tell the truth.

I will keep writing. *I am not afraid.*

And when life speeds up this hamster wheel of life in the USA, I get in my midnight blue car and listen to Los Alacranes's "México-Americano" and take refuge at a familiar place, where Ecetahl and Zephyrus, fly hand in hand and kiss my forehead. I visit a place—with no walls—that reaches inside me and tells me I belong. Reaching for the clouds above me, I kneel, sit down with my legs crossed, and dig my toes into the cold sand. While I sift sand through my fingers, I stare at the horizon, where water and sky press against each other.

As the salt-scented air consumes me and waves crash onto shore, with a branch, I carve my name—Sofía Martínez. Like always, my name curls upward wanting to fly away and then back. *What was it that the woman at the thrift store told me about my signature?* "The past is always present in your future." I finally understand the woman's soothsaying. "Your writing is legible. You've come to this world to communicate. Don't be afraid," she assured me. The woman had asked me if I was an artist or a writer—I am both. I paint the world with words.

The fire I carry inside will keep me warm. This evening the stars above me will blink and whisper words into my ears:

"Buenas noches, Chofi.

Good evening, Sofía.

It's time.

Are you ready?

¿Estás lista?

Xipatlani papalotl."

The sun, the moon, and the winds talk to me because I am Francisco and Helena's daughter—relative of the monarch butterflies, birds, and trees. I am listening. I have always been listening. I am the voices of my ancestors. I now know I have been chosen to travel long distances with all the monarch butterflies because I am a descendant of the butterfly people. Nobody tells us where to go; we have always known where to go for thousands and thousands of years.

From a distance, my relatives ask, "*Do you want to paint the world with words?*"

"Yes, yes, I will shape our stories with words even if they hurt in this infinite Dreamland where the past is always present in our future. *I am ready*," I answer as I hold on tight to the winged locket, where I placed Tío Miguel's photograph and carry his writer's spirit with me. *He's my San Miguel de Michoacán.*

I am not afraid to write because I can smell nectar from a distance. My enormous wings are orange crowned with black like my father and mother's. Reaching for the clouds, I extend my wings and listen to the world as I tilt my head back, taking in the beauty of the ever-changing sky, where purples, oranges, and pinks meet and dissolve into the dark blue of the night, where I can always fly with my freedom wings without anyone's permission in this limitless space for dream makers. In this place of dreams, I spread my wings and fly-sense as I uncurl my butterfly tongue and suck milkweed stories out of life. I open myself like a book and fly effortlessly. *Can you see me?* I will always be at this ever-changing place writing and dreaming with my eyes wide open, where dozens of white eyes on my monarch wings see the world from high above, always seeking and exposing the truth.

Sofía Martínez Ramírez "La Writer" c/s

ACKNOWLEDGEMENTS

To my mother, Estela, "Estelita" and my father, Francisco Gutiérrez, gracias por sus cuentos, lucesitas, y sonrisas. To my brothers, Francisco and Gastón, my superheroes, and their families, thank you, for being part of my journey. To my pareja, Paulino Azúcar Mendoza, for his love of soccer, which gave me time to write when our Zonia Quetzalli, our Quetzal, fell asleep. Deep gratitude to the man who taught me grammar, Professor William Salomone, to the man who introduced me to literature, Dr. Brent Gowen, and the man who introduced me to Chicano literature, Dr. Carlos von Son, R.I.P., Profe. Thank you to all the writers—living and deceased—who with their words on paper, taught me how to write and love writing.

My motivation to continue writing required a network of masa for tamales inspectors. Immense appreciation, to my sister, Mireya Gutiérrez-Agüero, who shared the earliest draft with close friends and family like she was the proud madrina of her sister's tamalito. Tomás H. Lucero, fellow poet, whose comments were a necessary tool to begin honing *Dreaming with Mariposas* (originally Kissing Dreams from a Distance and then Dream Makers). Tlazocamati Alejandro Meraz Chichiltekolotl for taking the time to discuss corn. My former Upward Bound students, Sarah Quiroz and Carolina Feria. Caro, while she was attending UC Santa Barbara, asked me if I could send her my stories to share them with her professor. Caro's interest reminded me for whom I was writing my novel—gracias Caro. To my godson, Sebastián Emiliano Agüero, my sister's son, *thank you* for reading *Dreaming with Mariposas*, Mijo.

Readers of the earliest draft also included Carlos Gómez, a colleague in the Spanish Department, at Palomar College, my junior high buddy, Genoveva Gómez, who found an old copy of the manuscript after I lost my USB drive with the revised version of the novel and my college buddy, Doris López Maciel, who read the original draft and encouraged me to finish the book. Sylvia Mendoza, friend and author of *The Book of Latina Women*, your writer's wisdom was essential for *Dreaming with Mariposas* to come to full fruition. Thank you, Alejandra Sánchez, for being an ambassador for Chicanx culture and literature, by supporting *Dreaming with Mariposas*. To my fellow writers, Walter Dutton, Zach Pugh, and Raymond Morris, for reading several vignettes during our Writers Workshops at our alma matter, California State University San Marcos. Muchas gracias to my Comadre Claudia León for sharing laughs and memories when we discussed the vignettes, "'Go back to Mexico!'" and "El Diablo." Gracias Adolfo Guzman-Lopez for taking my call to discuss journalism and *Dreaming with Mariposas*. Thank you Corie De Anda, Mario Martínez, Milly Coldwell, Olga Gutiérrez García, Sergio Vásquez, Matt Sedillo, Ozzie Monge, and David Hollingsworth for our charla(s) about *Dreaming with Mariposas*. Writer and poet, ire'ne lara silva, for inspiring my title and for her revision suggestions all the way from Austin, Texas.

Thank you to my Palomar College colleague, Dr. Michael James Lundell, for reading the manuscript and my MiraCosta

College colleagues, Francisco Álvarez, R.I.P., María Figueroa, and Karla Cordero, for expressing interest in *Dreaming with Mariposas*. Fellow colleagues and writers, John McGuinness and Dr. Darci Strother, thank you, *thank you*, immensely for your editing suggestions. Elva Cisneros, muchísimas gracias for reading the last drafts of *Dreaming with Mariposas* and your editor's eye. Publishers, William Harry Harding "Bill" and Lee Byrd, for your encouraging words. Thank you to Jennifer Baszile, author of *The Black Girl Next Door*, for coining "dream makers." Gracias Consuelo Martinez, Escondido's Deputy Mayor, for discussing time and my *Dreaming with Mariposas* cover letter. Gracias to California State University San Marcos colleague, Dr. Xuan Santos, for your Call for Submissions post via Facebook for La Chola Conference. Gracias a ti, Xuan, I wrote "Cholas Falsas." Gris Muñoz, a big warm thank you for believing in my manuscript and for your artistic eye all the way from El Paso, Texas. Mujer, con tus palabras me puse las pilas. Artesana, Mary Lou Valencia, thank you also for your artistic eye too, which allowed me to begin dreaming the cover. Xochi Small Bear, thank you for your literary consejos for the novel. Jo Reyes-Boitel, thank you so much for preparing *Dreaming with Mariposas* for steaming at FlowerSong Press and Edward Vidaurre, el publisher tamalero, for the delicious batches of libro tamales. And thank you to the creative spirit of the artisans of San Miguel de Allende, Guanajuato, México, for showing me the way. Much appreciation to everyone, including my Facebook family and friends, for your hearts, words of encouragement, shocked emoji, wishes, likes, and hearts, who believed in my first novel, *Dreaming with Mariposas*. Jorge Garza,

Qetza, thank you for your artistic spirit and giving *Dreaming with Mariposas* wings to fly. To all my nieces and nephews, this book is for you.

THANK YOU, *Dreaming with Mariposas*, for looking out for me and keeping me company during the Covid-19 2020 pandemic as a witness and Covid-19 survivor.

AFTERWORD

I started writing *Dreaming with Mariposas*, originally titled *Kissing Dreams from a Distance*, after the birth of my first-born, Zonia Quetzalli "Quetzal," in 2008, when she was about eight-months old, and I couldn't fall asleep thinking about writing—specifically my students' writing and my writing. That restless evening, I understood both nonfiction and creative writing would be ever present in my life.

While lying in bed, two thoughts kept eating at me: Virginia Woolf's "What will women's writing look like?" and Toni Morrison's "If there's a book you really want to read, but it hasn't been written yet, then you must write it." With those thoughts, I headed to the room I called office, painted a deep-sea blue with a poster of Che Guevara, walking arm in arm with two women comrades (long before his hands were cut and sent to Fidel Castro). On another wall hung a replica of Pablo Picasso's *Guernica*, mirroring the stories trapped in my mind I would one day paint with words in book form. I stared through a doorway with a missing door, a portal to the spirit world, at a black and white photograph of my maternal grandmother, Aurora Ramírez Cisneros, whom I never met, staring back with furrowed eyebrows.

Aurora Ramírez Cisneros, my maternal grandmother

Aurora. I said her name, and she lit the fire.

That is how my addiction to my second book, *Dreaming with Mariposas*, began—by listening to Virginia Woolf, Toni Morrison, and Sandra Cisneros and by capturing my ghosts. At night, as soon as our firstborn fell asleep, I became la bruja de la noche—and if I was lucky—sometimes del día. Very rarely though. At wee hours of the night, I flew with letters; I talked and listened to my fantasmitas. My ghosts. Night after night including on the weekends, they didn't stop coming. When I needed clarification, I talked to the living. Sometimes I'd be sitting at a restaurant and see a ghost on a person's face, and the story didn't disappear until my fingers trapped my vision on the computer screen.

To keep the energy of writers in the room, I surrounded myself with books, candles and photographs. Tomás Rivera's… *y no se lo tragó la tierra /. . . And the Earth Did Not Devour Him* and Sandra Cisneros's *The House on Mango Street* became my writing totems. The photographs of writers I had met in person, including Dr. Guillermo Marín, Victor Villaseñor, and Sandra Cisneros, I kept near my work area, to keep their flow in the room.

And then one day in 2010 I sat with two critics who read the manuscript. To my surprise, *Dreaming with Mariposas* took a hiatus for years because criticism I discovered had seeped into my creative process, leaving me impotent with my new-found genre. So, then I reconciled with my first love, Poetry, and promised myself to return to *Dreaming with Mariposas*.

Two years later when I returned to the manuscript, my USB's memory went blank and so did mine. I didn't cry over the loss of my USB drive since I had lost my mother in 2011, and Paulina Xitlalli, my secondborn daughter, had arrived; I knew tears were futile. In 2013, after reading Victor Martinez's *Parrot in the Oven*, a gift from fellow poet, John Martinez, at the 13 Poetas del Nuevo Sol/13 Poets of the New Sun in Boyle Heights, California, and the publication of my debut bilingual poetry collection, *Spider Woman / La Mujer Araña*, thanks to one of my Literary Santos, Victor Martinez's creative writing energy, I returned to the manuscript during summer and winter breaks. On one occasion, I googled Gabriel García Márquez and talked to his spirit too.

I am eternally indebted with the late Francisco X. Alarcón for taking me under his wing. He did not have an opportunity to read my manuscript. I promised him we would drive up north with the family and visit him to hand deliver the manuscript. Unfortunately, the man I consider my Chicano role model, Francisco X. Alarcón, passed away on January 15, 2016. I leave you reader with Alarcón's words he shared with poet, Iris De Anda, and me in Los Ángeles, California, at the National Immigrant Integration Conference in 2014 at the Los Angeles Convention Center, where we were keynote poets: "We are writing our stories, and they need to be heard. They have to publish our work. *It's important.*"

¡Tahui!
¡Tahui!
¡Tahui!
¡Tahui!

Sonia Gutiérrez
Escondido, California

ABOUT THE AUTHOR

Sonia Gutiérrez is the author of *Spider Woman / La Mujer Araña* (Olmeca Press, 2013) and the coeditor of *The Writer's Response* (Cengage Learning, 2016). She teaches critical thinking and writing, women's, gender, and sexuality studies, and multicultural studies. Her second bilingual poetry collection, *Paper Birds / Pájaros de papel*, is forthcoming in 2022. She is currently working on Sana Sana Colita de Rana, a poetry collection, and moderating Poets Responding. She lives in California with her family and cat, Arlito. To learn more about Sonia Gutiérrez and her work, visit *www.soniagutierrez.com*.

Earlier versions of vignettes appeared in literary magazines, journals, zines, websites, and anthologies:

"The Laundry Mat" (retitled "Launderland") in *Lavandería: A Mixed Load of Women, Wash, and Word*

"Rocky Girls" and "Green Dollar Dreams" in City Works Literary Journal

"El Huevo" in *Mujeres de Maiz: Flor y Canto: La Sagrada*

"El Huevo" in *Mujeres de Maiz: 13 Baktun: Return of the Wisdom of the Elders*

"Locked Up in the Mind," "El Borracho," "American Cats Mean More Than a Woman's Body," (retitled "A Woman's Body"), and "The Day Paco Almost Had a Heart Attack" (retitled "The Night Paco Almost Had a Heart Attack") in *AlternaCtive PublicaCtions*

"On Top of a Treetop" in *Chicana in the Midst*

"The Wind in My Hair," "Make Believe," and "La Migra Chasing My Mind" in *Hinchas de Poesía*

"The Wind in My Hair" in *Santanero #8*

"In the Time of Memories and Dreams" (Spanish translation, retitled "Dreaming with Aurora") in *Frontera Esquina*

"Freckled Like My Skin" (retitled "Helena's Frijoles de la Olla") in *La Palabra Enchilado: A Literary Café*

"The Grown Man" in *Unheard Voices of Redemption*

"Tomasito," "Mother and Her Scissors," "A Window of Her Own" in *Storyacious: Feasting on Stories*

"Las Muy Muy," "La Tamalera," and "Alicia in the Company of Men" in *Huizache: The Magazine of Latino Literature*

"Big Bad Wolves" and "In the Time of Memories and Dreams"

(retitled "Dreaming with Aurora") in *Sunshine Noir II*

"Freckled Like My Skin" (retitled "Helena's Frijoles de la Olla"), "The Mango and Mambo Days," and "The Story of the First Year" in *Puro Chicanx Writers of the 21st Century*

"Sofía, ¿qué soñaste?" and "Dreaming with Aurora" forthcoming in *The Dreaming Machine*

"Cholas Falsas" forthcoming at MiraCosta College's La Chola Conference

Sonia Gutiérrez and Her Literary Predecessors

Francisco Gutiérrez, Dr. Guillermo Marín, Sonia Gutiérrez, and Mireya Gutiérrez-Agüero. Photograph courtesy of Pablo Salgado, 1998

Paulino Azúcar Mendoza, Mireya Gutiérrez-Agüero, Victor Villaseñor, and Sonia Gutiérrez. Photograph courtesy of Calvin OneDeer, 2001

Sonia Gutiérrez and Sandra Cisneros
Photograph courtesy of the Escondido Public Library Staff,
2007

Sonia Gutiérrez, Francisco X. Alarcón, and Abel Salas
Photograph courtesy of Paulino Azúcar Mendoza, 2012

GROUP DISCUSSION QUESTIONS

1. Why do you believe Sonia Gutiérrez titled her book, *Dreaming with Mariposas*, instead of *Dreaming with Butterflies*?

2. In "Rocky Girls," Chofi tells the reader her father teaches her sister, Paloma, and her boxing. Why do you believe Francisco teaches his daughters to box?

3. Identify a persistent theme in *Dreaming with Mariposas*. Select several vignettes and explain the author's purpose.

4. To the Martínez family, the realm of dreams is as important as reality. What does your family believe about dreams? Does your family interpret dreams?

5. The reader learns Sofía's father, Francisco, drinks and performs toxic masculinity. Do Mexican, American, and/or any other culture, condone toxic behavior in boys and men?

6. There are several instances in the novel, where Sofía thinks critically. Who teaches Sofía to think critically? *Do you think critically?*

7.   In *Dreaming with Mariposas*, Sofía complains about her family's strict gender roles. She does not want to wash or iron her parents' clothing; instead, she wants to mow the lawn. If you did not have to conform to society's expectations, what would you choose to do and not do? Why?

8.   In the novel, the author mentions Helena's "herb-filled cabinets." Does your family concoct an herbal remedy that heals an ailment? Where did the remedy originate?

9.   In *Dreaming with Mariposas*, Paloma and Sofía create an altar for their Abuelita Aurora. How does your family honor your ancestors?

10. In Gutiérrez's vignette, "In the Place of Dreams," what does the character learn about college?

11. Even though her parents are illiterate, Sofía knows she will go to college because her parents instill those expectations. Who first told you that you were going to college?

12. In the vignette, "Tomasito," readers learn about Tomasito, Simón, and Víctor. Reflect on your high school experience. How did teenage students treat LGBTQ+ students at your high school?

13. In the novel, Mr. Goldberg claims Paloma and Sofía are cholas, and Sofía tells the reader in "Locked Up in the Mind" she is not afraid of her cousin, Beto, who *is* a cholo. Do you know anyone like Beto who is stuck in the school-to-prison pipeline? Is the person's experience similar to or different from Beto's experience?

14. By the end of the novel, Sofía is horrified about the femicide of women in Ciudad Juárez, México. Has the femicide problem receded? Where else in the world do femicides occur?

15. How does Gutiérrez present the body as a conflict zone, meaning who controls the body, and why are bodies controlled?

16. In the novel, the author presents monarch butterflies and birds as metaphors. What does Helena teach her daughter about the symbiotic relationship between humans and nature? Be specific.

17. In the vignette, "La Tamalera," the reader learns food is important and sacred to the Martínez family. Sofía narrates her family's tradition of making tamales. What important food in your family has been passed down intergenerationally to you? Is it gender inclusive?

18.
    Pretend you are Sofía Martínez Ramírez "La Writer." What problem(s) at the local, state, national, and/or global level would you write about? Why?

19. What important lesson does the character, Tía Alicia, in "The Story of the First Year" share with the reader?

20. In college, Sofía discovers writing is her superpower. What is your superpower?

21. The author integrates Spanish, Spanglish, and Nahuatl in her novel, *Dreaming with Mariposas*. Why do you believe the author includes these three languages in her novel?

22. The author includes photographs to honor her grandmother and her literary predecessors. Do photographs inspire you to persevere and fulfill your goals and dreams?

23. In a Gutierrezesque literary style, write a vignette about a memory in your life.

24. Analyze a recurrent rhetorical strategy in *Dreaming with Mariposas*. How does it enrich Gutiérrez's novel?

25. Select a problem Sofía Martínez "La Writer" recounts in *Dreaming with Mariposas*. What can be done to fix the problem?

26. If you could meet Sofía, what questions would you ask her?

27.   If you were placed in the Martínez sisters' dire situation, such as in the vignette, "The Night Paco Almost Had a Heart Attack," what would you do?

28.   If you could meet the author, Sonia Gutiérrez, what would you ask her?